Moray

40 Coast and Country Walks

The author and publisher have made every effort to ensure that the information in this publication is accurate, and accept no responsibility whatsoever for any loss, injury or inconvenience experienced by any person or persons whilst using this book.

published by
pocket mountains ltd
The Old Church, Annanside,
Moffat DG10 9HB

ISBN: 978-1-9070251-3-6

Printed in Poland

Introduction

This book covers the southern coastline of the Moray Firth, from just east of Inverness to the North Sea at Rattray Head. The area includes Nairn, the whole of Moray, including Forres, Dufftown, Buckie and Elgin, and the picturesque fishing villages of North Aberdeenshire such as Gardenstown, Crovie and Pennan. In addition to the coast, with its vast sandy beaches and intricate rock formations, cliffs and coves, the landscape extends inland towards the fringes of the Cairngorms. Here are the moors and glens, habitat of red deer and golden eagle, and the heartland of malt whisky – Speyside.

Such variety makes for a fascinating range of walks which pass distilleries, scout out the Moray Firth dolphins, hike across rolling farmland and gentle moors, watch red squirrels and birds amongst the pines and dunes of the coast, and explore some of Scotland's most picturesque villages with tiny cottages hemmed in between the cliffs and the sea.

Using this guide

This guide contains 40 short to moderate walks, most of which can be undertaken in half a day. Whilst many follow prepared and waymarked paths, some cross open hills or moor which can be boggy or steep. Although the area is known for its good sunshine record, the weather can be changeable, with cold winds and often heavy snowfall in the winter. Most of the walks require waterproof footwear and clothing. A sketch map accompanies each route, but walkers should also carry an OS map to aid navigation on all but the most straightforward routes.

The few walks that are suitable for all-terrain baby buggies are highlighted at the start of the relevant routes. Many routes are, however, ideal for well-clad families, including beaches at Burghead Bay and Cullen, red squirrel-spotting at Culbin and Roseisle and a mountain challenge for little legs on Ben Aigan. On walks starting from towns or forestry car parks, there are often toilets and picnic and/or barbeque facilities nearby.

Public transport is relatively good in the well-connected corridor linking Inverness to Aberdeen. The railway stops at main towns, including Nairn, Forres, Elgin and Huntly, while local bus services give access to many of the walks. There are also cycle tracks which can be used to reach some walks, whilst the Keith and Dufftown Heritage Railway runs vintage diesel trains during summer weekends and could be used for walks at Keith, Drummuir and Dufftown.

Access and dogs

The Land Reform (Scotland) Act 2003 gave walkers the right of access over most Scottish land away from residential buildings. With this right comes responsibilities, as set out in the Scottish Outdoor Access Code, essentially requiring respect for other land users and responsible access, especially on farmed and grazing land. In particular, dogs should be kept on tight leads during the spring and early summer to stop them disturbing groundnesting birds and farm livestock. Dogs should also be kept well away from sheep with lambs at all times. Some of the moorland routes are used for grouse-shooting. Ticks and midges can be a hazard in summer; take precautions such as covering up, wearing light-coloured clothing, using insect repellent and removing ticks each day, especially if the walk leads through bracken.

History

Moray and North Aberdeenshire have a long history of human habitation. Until the 10th century, small farming communities of Picts lived here in a loose affiliation of tribes – Pictavia. They have left a variety of archaeological remains, including the impressive Suenos Stone on the outskirts of Forres. Along the coast, the Pictish ritual of the burning of the Clavie continues in Burghead to protect fishing boats for the coming year. Route markers on the Burghead Bay walk show the Burghead Bull, found on carved slabs during the excavation of the largest Pictish fort in Scotland which overlooks the sea from the fishing port.

As Pictavia became Scotland, castles, forts and religious buildings began to dot the landscape. Elgin Cathedral and nearby Spynie Palace were once the seats of the Bishops of Moray, dating back to the early 13th century. The cathedral was known as 'the Lantern of the North' because of its free-standing appearance across the flat plains. In 1390, well before the Scottish Reformation, the cathedral and much of the burgh of Elgin was sacked and burned by Alexander Stewart, the Earl of Buchan, who became known as the Wolf of Badenoch. The fourth son of King Robert II, Alexander presided over a vast swathe of country and frequently came into conflict with the Bishops of Moray. His ex-communication from the church led to the brutal Elgin attack. Although repairs were undertaken in the 15th and 16th centuries, it is as a spectacular ruin that it stands today. Closer to Forres are the Cistercian and Benedictine monasteries of Kinloss and Pluscarden – the latter having been restored and reinhabited with monks from Prinknash Abbey in Wiltshire in 1948.

Local industry

The local economy has long relied on the three Fs – farming, fishing and forestry. The effect of the Gulf Stream on the Moray Firth creates a relatively dry and sunny micro-climate which, combined with the fertile soils of the Laich, means Moray and North Aberdeenshire produce significant crops of cereals, soft fruit and vegetables. It is said that before sandstorms destroyed the village of Nevistoun at Culbin, citrus fruit were grown in almost Mediterranean conditions here. Eastwards, villages with access to the deep sea fishing grounds have been dominated by fishing, though most of the trawlers have been replaced by leisure craft; further east at Peterhead fishing still dominates and in Cullen, this heritage is preserved in the delicious Cullen Skink, a creamy soup of potato and smoked fish.

All this food required something to wash it down with, and the geography obliged, being perfect for the production of *Uisge Beatha* – the Water of Life, or whisky. It is thought that the art of distilling was brought to Scotland by St Patrick, who landed in Kintyre in the 5th century; the first official record of large-scale production is from 1494. By this time, small-scale stills were operating in many parts of the region, particularly the foothills of the Cairngorms. Production was given a boost by the dissolution of the monasteries in the 15th century as the monks knew how to distil and often put that knowledge to good use. The introduction of taxes on both malt and the finished product in the late 17th century hailed the start of the whisky smuggling industry, and by the 1820s, it was estimated that more than half of all whisky produced in Scotland was evading the eyes of the government. Soon after, the tax laws were changed to make legal production profitable – many of today's distilleries were established on the site of illicit stills. Whisky remains a key product for Scotland, with the Speyside area of Moray as its heartland.

As well as an army of excise men, the region has been a stronghold of the English and then British armed forces since the defeat of the Jacobites at Culloden in 1746. Fort George, the impressive six-sided fort jutting into the Moray Firth from a headland near Ardesier, was completed in 1769 as one of a number of forts along the Great Glen. Built with the purpose of subduing the Scots once and for all, no shot has ever been fired from its ramparts as by the time it was completed the Jacobite rebellion was over. However, it served as an important recruiting and training base for the thousands of Scottish recruits to the British Army during the days of the Empire and still houses a large garrison today as the home of the Black Watch, 3rd Battalion, Royal Regiment of Scotland.The geographic position of the Moray and North Aberdeenshire coast has been vital to the defence of Britain in more recent years. The RAF bases at Lossiemouth and Kinloss were set up in 1938 as the threat of World War II loomed and, despite recent cutbacks, the two bases still employ more than 6000 staff.

Natural history

This diverse area supports a wide range of species. Most famous are the Moray Firth dolphins, one of only two sizeable British colonies of bottlenose dolphins, with several walks offering a good chance to spot them. The Whale and Dolphin Conservation Society's information centre at Spey Bay is also a good place to spot migrating wildfowl and waders. At nearby Findhorn, osprey can be observed from a hide. Along much of the coast are dunes and pine forest where the red squirrel makes its home. Evidence of much older wildlife can be found near Hopeman, where fossil dinosaur footprints are displayed by the trail.

A mere 26km from Inverness, Nairn is the first major settlement as you head east along the Moray Firth coastline. The Duke of Cumberland is supposed to have stayed here on the eve of the notorious Battle of Culloden. Nairn was established as a fishing port and market town, divided into separate Gaelic- and Scots-speaking communities; the divide can still be seen in the contrast between the cramped cottages huddled into the harbourside and Fishertown and the long main street and elegant villas of the West End.

Nairn was early to capitalise on the burgeoning tourist industry brought by the railway in the 1860s. The town became a popular resort, with rows of Victorian bathing machines depositing bathers into the bracing waters whilst preserving their modesty. As well as the sea, said to have healing properties at the time of the August harvest, golf also brought visitors to the town and has remained a popular draw, with three courses. In the 1970s Charlie Chaplin was a regular visitor, taking a daily walk along the seafront. The actress Tilda Swinton – a local resident – has maintained the cinematic theme by establishing a quirky annual film festival based here.

Today, it is mainly leisure boats which sail from the harbour to join the dolphins in the Moray Firth. Whilst the coast remains a great attraction with fine views across the water to the Black Isle and the distant mountains, the inland forests and the castles at Brodie and Cawdor provide an excellent contrast and a good chance to combine a walk with an historic tour.

6

In and around Nairn

Whiteness Head

bothy

construction yard
(disused)

Carse of
Ardersier

Whiteness Head from Nairn

Distance 16.5km **Time** 4 hours (including return) **Terrain** good paths and tracks, pebbly and sandy shore; depending on the state of the tide, either the outward or return leg can be walked along the beach **Map** OS Explorer 422 **Access** regular buses and trains to Nairn on the Inverness-Aberdeen route

Stretching west from Nairn a long pebble and sandy shore leads out to a spit, where there's a good chance of spotting seals, dolphins and seabirds. A long but level walk with plenty of interest and good views across the Moray Firth.

Start from the leisure centre on Marine Road Central, on the north side of Nairn, where there is parking. From here, walk left onto the Promenade Walk along the coast. The beach and the town were developed as a resort during Victorian times. Horse-drawn bathing machines would have been a common sight on the sands as they wheeled Victorian ladies into the water to allow them to bathe without being seen.

However, the popularity of these waters dates back to pre-industrial times when the Lammas tide, coinciding with a festival to celebrate the first fruits of the summer harvest, was said to have healing properties.

Whiteness Head is the extreme end of this stretch of beach, and it is possible at low tide to complete the walk entirely on the shore. However, the first part of the outward journey described here travels inland; this alternative adds variety to an otherwise linear route and can be used if the tide is too high on the outward or return walk.

Once past the golf course clubhouse, the route carries on between the course and the sea for a short distance before a signed route turns

Seafront

Delnies circular footpath 6 miles

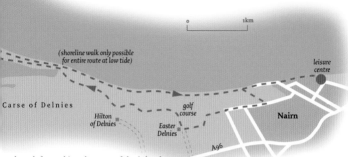

0   1km

(shoreline walk only possible
for entire route at low tide)

leisure
centre

Carse of Delnies

Hilton
of Delnies

golf
course

Easter
Delnies

Nairn

A96

sharp left, marking the start of the inland section. The path cuts across a couple of holes, so take care, give way to any golfers and don't disturb the play. At Altonburn Road, turn right to pass houses and a hotel. At the end of the road turn left (SP Delnies Circular); the path soon bears right, skirting along field edges and tracks to Easter Delnies Farm. Beyond the barns, a track branches right downhill past the house entrance towards the hedge which borders the golf course. Turning left at the hedge, a path takes you along the field edge at first but later across rough grass and gorse.

At a junction after a footbridge, continue ahead onto the main track (the left branch leads to Hilton of Delnies Farm). After crossing a flat area of carseland, the track runs close to the pebble embankment on the shoreline. You can either cross this onto the beach, turning left to continue to the point, or carry on along the track until it peters out after eventually passing a bothy, where you then take to the shore.

As the pebble and sand beach becomes a narrow spit, it attracts many seabirds eager to forage for the creatures along the tideline. Seals sometimes haul out on the sands, although they are more likely to watch you from the water. Over to the left, beyond the bothy, is the deep water inlet and old industrial site used to build North Sea oil platforms which is to be redeveloped as a marina and housing. The point itself is a great spot to look out for the bottle-nose dolphins that swim up and down the Moray Firth on a daily basis. The 130-strong colony is the second largest in the UK. If you have no luck spotting them here or at Spey Bay, there are almost guaranteed daily sightings at Chanonry Point near Rosemarkie on the Black Isle opposite, where the creatures come in very close to the shore in their search for salmon on the rising tide.

From Whiteness Head, you can either return all the way to Nairn along the shore or take the inland option already described. Keep an eye out for what must be one of Britain's most low-lying trig points, half hidden amongst the gorse on the right side of the track as you walk back.

Nairn to Cawdor by the river

Distance 9km (one way) **Time** 2 hours
Terrain clear path, narrow and rough at
times, can be impassable when river is in
spate **Map** OS Explorer 422 **Access** regular
buses and trains to Nairn on the
Inverness-Aberdeen route, bus from
Cawdor (schooldays and times only)

**This riverside walk links the seaside town
of Nairn and Cawdor where a visit to the
castle – or the excellent village teashop –
complete the day before taking the mid-
afternoon bus or walking back to Nairn.**

The best parking for this walk is at the
long stay car park opposite the harbour,
temptingly named The Maggot after the
foul-smelling stagnant water that used to
pool here: follow the road signs to reach
it. From here, walk upstream beside the
River Nairn, soon passing under the main
road. Ignore the bridges and keep on the
path to Cawdor on the left.

If staying in Nairn or arriving by public
transport, begin by heading up the High
Street and, three-quarters of the way along,
turning left into Church Street. After 200m,
another left leads into Church Road,
passing the old cemetery and site of
Nairn's first church. Bear right around the
cemetery to reach the riverbank and turn
right to walk upstream. Keeping on the
riverside path, do not cross Jubilee Bridge
but wait until the second footbridge,
Firhall, and cross here, turning right on the
far side to join the route from the Maggot
and follow the path signed for Cawdor.

Enjoy the pleasant banks of the River
Nairn, popular with salmon and trout
fishermen before joining the road at
Howford Bridge. Don't cross this lovely old

straight on at the junction and turn left onto the track. Keep left at the fork to soon reach the confluence with the Cawdor Burn. The path accompanies the burn; look out for the signed path to Cawdor on the left, then turn right onto the road towards the centre of this small village.

Cawdor is synonymous with Macbeth, even though he acceded to the Scottish throne in 1040, following Duncan's death at nearby Elgin Castle, whilst Cawdor wasn't even built until the 14th century. Shakespeare is responsible for this historical anomaly, titling Macbeth the Thane of Cawdor and leaving today's visitors to imagine the vengeful Lady Macbeth haunting the corridors of the present-day castle. Whilst the Macbeth connection is played down, Cawdor Castle is well worth a visit to explore the labyrinth of rooms and informal gardens. A refreshing twist is given by the amusing personal notes from the current owners which are dotted about, reinforcing the fact that this is a family home rather than a managed heritage site. Cawdor's other attraction is the Village Green tearoom. Housed in a small interiors shop, it provides a good opportunity to refuel before the return walk or to wait for the bus back to Nairn.

bridge but rejoin the grassy path on the far side of the main road to soon shadow the riverbank once more. After Graeme's Pool, named in memory of a young local angler, the path leaves the riverside to follow a small ridge overlooking farmland. Keep on the main path, eventually reaching a kissing gate to return to the riverside. This section can flood when the water level is very high, but more usually is just a little muddy underfoot. Follow the white arrow

Culbin Sands and Kingsteps

Distance **10km** Time **2 hours 30**
Terrain **sandy shore and dunes, forest
paths and tracks, minor road; waymarking
on some sections** Map **OS Explorer 422**
Access **regular buses and trains to Nairn
on the Inverness-Aberdeen route**

**Explore the coast immediately east of
Nairn, reaching the dunes and pines of
Culbin Forest before heading through
farmland to return via the long expanse of
sandy beach.**

The walk begins from the enticingly-
named Maggot car park opposite the
harbour; follow signs from the main road.
If walking from the town centre, head
towards the harbour and then cross the
footbridge to reach the car park on the far
side.This area was once a tidal creek used
for mooring boats before being filled and

used as a drying green for washing by
nearby residents, finally being made into a
recreation ground and car park. From here,
aim straight for the sea, looking out for
any dolphins that sometimes play in the
harbour entrance at high tide.

As soon as you can, turn right onto the
expansive sands. Across the water, the high
cliffs at Nigg dominate the horizon; take
care not to venture far out across the sand
as the tide can rush in very quickly and
people have been stranded here. Further
along the beach, a curious pattern of low
posts project from the sand. Although they
look as though they were designed to fell
unsuspecting toddlers not watching where
they are running, they are, in fact, anti-
glider posts erected during the Second
World War. Army generals were convinced
that the Scottish northeast coast was the

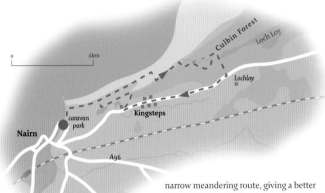

obvious landing area for an invasion from the continent and a rigorous line of defences was built, including vast lines of tank traps, pill boxes and these anti-glider posts – intended to stop a glider from being able to land.

The pines of Culbin Forest draw nearer and eventually a burn blocks the way along the beach. Walk inland for a short distance to reach a rickety bridge (or it may be possible to cross the outflow on the beach at low tide). Take the faint path through the gorse and broom before heading inland across the saltmarsh, aiming for the trees to reach a good path. Bear left onto this and follow it for 250m, keeping a sharp eye out for a path coming down from the forest on the right. Climb up the steps here and plunge into the dense forest, continuing ahead and then turning left onto a clear track. The next path on the left provides an optional detour along a

narrow meandering route, giving a better feel for the forest and a chance of spotting red squirrels. Otherwise, stay on the main track to reach Junction 23, where you turn right. The forest was planted to stabilise the shifting dunes and is laid out in regimented blocks with each junction numbered – despite this, it is still possible to get lost and without a map showing the location of each junction, it is surprisingly hard to find your way!

After a gate, the track meets a road; turn right to follow this past Druim and then the small village of Kingsteps with its ever-growing array of *Grand Designs*-style houses. As the road descends, look out for the lane on the right, signed for Fisherman's Bothy. Go through the car park onto a lane and fork left to pick up a sandy path aiming for the coast. At Minister's Pool, turn left onto the main path to Nairn, passing the golf course and emerging into the car park at Nairn East Beach. You can either cross the dunes to return over sand or follow the road through the caravan park to get back to the start.

Culbin Forest and the Hill 99 Trail

Distance 6km **Time** 1 hour 30
Terrain clear waymarked paths, suitable
for some all-terrain buggies if you don't
mind the odd grounding in the sand
Map OS Explorer 423 **Access** no public
transport to start

**This waymarked walk gives a great
introduction to the expanse of the Culbin
Forest and its dunes. Climb a high
wooden tower to scan over the treetops
and spot dolphins in the Moray Firth.**

The Culbin dune system is one of the
largest in the UK, extending over 7km and
including a wide sand bar which juts out
into the Moray Firth. The most dramatic
views are from the air and, as a private
aeroplane or helicopter is beyond the
means of most of us, the Forestry

Commission has provided the next best
thing – a giant wooden structure that
towers over the forest and will delight
children. The route to it is waymarked Hill
99, with black arrows from the Wellhill car
park; this is signed from the A96.

Start by taking the track from the
information board, passing a tree planted
by the then prime minister Harold Wilson
in 1969. The sight of this tree will make any
40-plus walkers feel old as the tree seems
remarkably mature and wrinkled – maybe
it was getting on a bit when it was
planted? Stay on the main track until a
signed right turn leads to the old gravel
pits. Now an oasis for waterbirds and rare
mosses, this area was once used to extract
the large deposits of gravel and sand that
lie beneath the ground. Follow the path

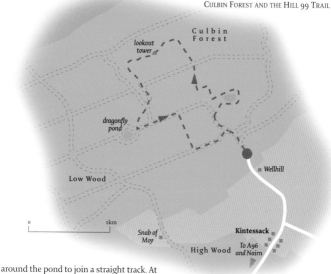

around the pond to join a straight track. At the crossroads, turn right and continue straight on at the next junction. The forest covers a huge area, criss-crossed by identical-looking forestry tracks, so every junction has been numbered to make navigation easier and you can pick up a map of them all in the car park.

Keep on the main path when it curves left for the short climb to the top of Culbin's highest point. The top of a former dune, Hill 99 does have a trig point marking its summit a mighty 25m above sea level. You can get much higher, however, by climbing the steps of the wooden tower. The expanse of saltmarsh and sand bars that make up the Culbin Sands Nature Reserve can be seen at the edge of the pines, as well as Tarbat Ness and perhaps even distant Morven on the

other side of the Moray Firth, while looking inland are the distant Cairngorms.

Drop downhill past the trig point to go straight on at Junction 45 and continue until you reach Junction 40. Aim right onto a smaller path. When this comes to another junction, you can make a short detour opposite to the dragonfly pond where these bright blue and green creatures skim the surface during the summer. Otherwise, turn left, following the waymarker onto a wide track through a younger section of the forest.

At Junction 42, branch left, looking out for a right turn onto a sandy path which eventually rejoins the main track near the start. Go right here to soon return to the car park.

◀ The Hill 99 viewpoint tower

Darnaway Forest and the River Findhorn

Distance **3.5km** Time **1 hour 30**
Terrain **woodland paths, steep drops to
gorge, care needed with children**
Maps **OS Explorer 423 and 419**
Access **no public transport to start**

**This beautiful walk through varied
woodland runs along the rim of a
precipitous gorge, allowing views down to
the winding River Findhorn below.**

Darnaway Forest lies to the southeast of
Nairn and is best approached by following
the signs south from the A96 near Brodie.
A minor road passes through Conicavel;
some distance further on, the parking area
is signed up to the left at a bend in the
road. This circuit heads through the trees
and along the Findhorn Gorge. Take the
path from the information board at the
parking area to cross a small footbridge.

At a track, turn left and follow it as it
curves right and comes to a T-junction.
Turn left again here, dropping steeply
downhill and eventually zigzagging down
steps with good views over the Dunearn
Burn and then the River Findhorn below.
The path now runs along the wooded lip
of the gorge, shadowing the River
Findhorn upstream.

Darnaway Forest has been here for more
than a thousand years and once played
host to royal hunting parties. Moray
Estates, which owns the forest as well as a
large number of farms and properties in
the area, can draw its history directly back
to Lord James Stewart, who ruled Scotland
following the defeat of Mary Queen of
Scots in 1568 until his assassination two
years later. As thanks for his advice and
support, Mary Queen of Scots made her

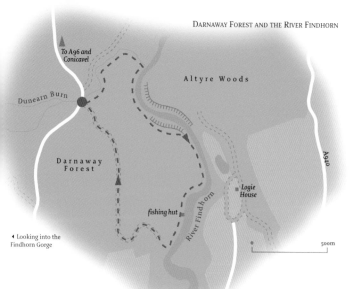

◄ Looking into the
Findhorn Gorge

half brother, James, the Earl of Moray
and gifted much of the land which forms
the bulk of the Moray Estates today.
The estate estimates that the oldest tree
growing here is more than 750 years old.
Although most of the forest is now made
up of commercial conifers – a mix of Scots
pine, Sitka spruce and Douglas fir – the
area around this walk has much more
native beech and oak.

The path requires care as it is bordered
by vertical drops to the swirling waters
below. A path off to the right makes for a
much shorter route back to the car park,
but for the full walk continue ahead. In a
couple of places steps lead down to fishing
spots where fly fisherman stand in the
cold waters hoping to tempt salmon
before retreating to the comfort of the

nearby fishing hut which is soon reached.
Pass in front of the hut and stay on the
path rather than taking the track.

After passing a large pool far below, the
white walls of Logie House can be seen
across the water. If time allows, Logie
Steading, just along from the house,
makes a good place to visit with the
chance to refuel on homemade cake, poke
around a couple of interesting shops and
de-bounce any children at the play area –
it is just off the A940 heading to Forres.

Turn right up wooden steps to leave the
gorge and at the track turn left and keep
left at the next junction. Stay on the main
track, ignoring any side routes and soon
you'll find yourself back by the parking
area at the start.

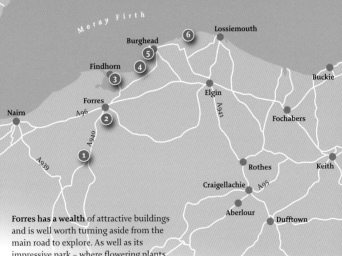

Forres has a wealth of attractive buildings and is well worth turning aside from the main road to explore. As well as its impressive park – where flowering plants are manipulated into ever more ambitious shapes – don't miss the Suenos Stone, a massive carved standing stone dating back to Pictish times and found on the eastern side of town.

The neighbouring coast and countryside has plenty to offer the walker and visitor. At the mouth of the river is the popular village of Findhorn, the western end of a spectacular beach. To the back of the beach, the former Roseisle dunes are now clothed in pinewoods, popular with picnicking families sharing space with scampering red squirrels. The fishing villages of Burghead and Hopeman provide plenty of interest and are linked by lovely cliffs and sandy bays, where it is always worth keeping an eye out for the passing dolphins; the finest walk heads right through to Lossiemouth.

Above Forres, the River Findhorn heads down from its source amongst the outliers of the Cairngorm mountains to bring clear water through a series of fine gorges. A new long-distance walk, the Dava Way, now provides a walking and cycling link between Forres and Grantown-on-Spey in the Cairngorms National Park. Following a disused railway line, the 38km route has been established through the hard work of volunteers and offers an excellent one- or two-day hike, including a crossing of little-visited Dava Moor and a grand viaduct. The Dava Way links with the Speyside Way and the Moray Coast Trail to create a circular route, the Moray Way, offering a week's walking and a great chance to discover every facet of Moray.

Findhorn Bay from Burghead beach ▶

Forres and Findhorn

Randolph's Leap from Logie Steading

Distance 4km **Time** 1 hour
Terrain good waymarked path, narrow in places with unprotected drops; very short section on minor road
Maps OS Explorer 419 and 422
Access no public transport

Venture along the wooded lip of the Findhorn Gorge to reach Randolph's Leap, scene of a courageous escape. This walk is popular with children, no doubt in part down to the excellent play area and café at the start point, Logie Steading. Care is needed near the rim of the gorge.

Logie Steading is 10km south of Forres, signed from the A940 and just off the B9007. Originally the home farm steading for the Logie Estate, the buildings now house a number of independent shops as well as a visitor centre with information about the River Findhorn and the walk.

There is also a walled garden, children's play area, toilets and a farm shop. To begin, walk past the play area and along a path next to the tall hedge. The large white building down the valley is Logie House which is privately owned.

The path bears left and there is the chance to crawl through a couple of living willow tunnels if such a desire seizes you. At the fork, follow the arrow sign to the right to reach a viewpoint over the River Findhorn below. As the path leads you upstream, ignore the signed path for Logie Steading, which is used on the return, and keep between the fence and steep bank.

After passing a deep pool of still water, you come to the Meeting of the Waters. Here, the Rivers Divie and Findhorn crash together by a massive rock which juts defiantly into their path. Carry on beside the Divie to reach the road where you turn

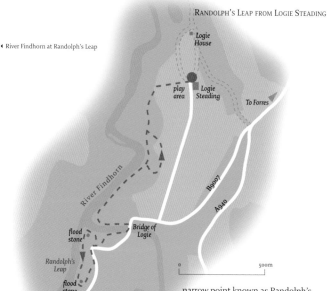

◄ River Findhorn at Randolph's Leap

right to cross the bridge. Take the path on the right-hand side of the road; this soon nears the road again at a map. Turn right here to follow the steps, keeping right at the fork to return to the confluence of the rivers, this time between them. Notice the commemorative stone – this was erected to mark the extent of the 'Muckle Flood' of 1829, the worst ever recorded, when the Findhorn raged 16m above its normal level after three days of continuous rain and flooded much of the lower valley.

Keep to the path as it heads upstream above high cliffs, carrying straight on where a path leaves to the left, to reach the narrow point known as Randolph's Leap. Despite the name, Randolph, the Earl of Moray in the 14th century, did not actually make the leap. Instead, the feat was undertaken by four members of the Cumming clan fleeing an ambush by Randolph during a bitter feud between local landowners.

From here, the path veers slightly away from the river and then bears left to pass a second flood stone. The main path returns to the road; walk left along this to the bend and pick up the path on the left near the map used on the way out to return to the bridge over the Divie. Retrace your steps onto the left-hand path down the Divie. Eventually, the sign for Logie Steading points right and the arrow signs will guide you back to the start.

Sanquhar Loch and the Nelson Tower

Distance 6.5km Time 2 hours Terrain clear, waymarked paths, tracks and roads with pavement; steep climb to tower
Map OS Explorer 423 Access regular buses and trains to Forres on the Inverness-Aberdeen route

Forres has some splendid buildings and parks, and this circuit selects the highlights for a short family-friendly walk.

The walk starts in Grant Park just east of the town centre off Victoria Road; there is a car park, signed for Nelson Tower. From the back of the car park, follow the track with the park on your right, soon climbing up steps that lead into the woods to the left. At a track, turn briefly left and then right up more steps to gain a higher track. A left turn onto this takes you across the wooded slopes of Cluny Hill. The Nelson Tower sits proudly out of sight on the summit and can be visited at the end of the walk. Ignoring the first left turn, take a

sharp waymarked left further on. At the next junction, turn right along an avenue of conifers; on the right is a depression known ominously as Helgy's Hole.

Keep right near some buildings before reaching a crossroads, where you drop left on what soon becomes a surfaced lane and emerges on St Leonard's Road, the location of some of Forres' more prestigious houses. Cross the road and take the track opposite, soon narrowing to a path between houses. Just before the path reaches a residential street, turn left into the woods and then right down steps to reach the picturesque Mosset Burn. This leads you to the right, where it soon widens into Sanquhar Loch.

Beyond the parking area, turn left along the road to pass the outflow, where you're likely to be pursued by hungry ducks accustomed to visitors armed with bread. Before the first house, turn left along a path which climbs above the loch. At a

Fishing platform, Sanquhar Loch

fork, branch right to join a track which soon crosses a minor road and leads into Sanquhar Woods. This is a peaceful section where you may spot deer, squirrels and woodland birds. Keep an eye out for the waymarks and take the third turning on the left to climb through the mixed woodland. A waymarked right turn takes you along the edge of the woods with views over the neighbouring farmland.

After zigzagging downhill to cross a pretty wooden footbridge and up the bank beyond, turn left along the top of the bank to reach Chapelton Farm, passing a lovely galleried barn on the left. Keep ahead onto the surfaced road to meet St Leonard's Road opposite the ornate Leanchoil Hospital building. Turn right along the pavement and verge, then left just beyond the last house, crossing the car park to reach a track into Muiry Wood.

Keeping to the waymarkers, turn left onto a path which winds through Scots pines, left again at a crossroads and finally left at a T-junction. There is now a straight section with glimpses towards Findhorn and the Moray Firth. Continue ahead alongside some houses to emerge at the cemetery. Bear right here, taking the road uphill but looking for a signed path on the left after passing between stone walls.

Soon this path rejoins the outward route; turn right and then sharp right again to return. If you wish to visit the Nelson Tower, then before descending the steps on the right continue ahead on a track until a left turn rises to the tower, a prominent Forres landmark. Open to the public during summer afternoons, the ascent of the 96 steps inside the white hexagonal tower is rewarded with fabulous views to the coast and inland towards the Cairngorms. The tower commemorates Nelson's victory at the Battle of Trafalgar. Afterwards, head back the way you came, descending the two sets of steps to return to the car park.

23

Findhorn explorer

Distance 4.5km **Time** 1 hour 15
Terrain waterside path, shoreline near
deep water with strong currents, beach
and minor road with pavement
Map OS Explorer 423 **Access** regular
bus from Forres

A popular circuit from the pretty village of
Findhorn, taking in the riverside, shore,
beach and dunes. The route can easily be
combined with a visit to the heritage
centre, a café, the Findhorn Foundation,
or all three.

Findhorn sits adjacent to the massive
bowl of slow-moving water that the River
Findhorn fills before finally reaching the
sea. This picturesque village with its
popular cafés, pubs and heritage centre is
popular at weekends with visitors walking
their dogs and children or messing about
on all sorts of boats. The cycle route from

Findhorn to nearby Forres provides an
alternative transport option if you have the
time. If driving, continue through the
village, following the signs for the heritage
centre, to the West Dunes car park. From
here, walk back along the road to pass the
icehouse, which forms part of the heritage
centre with a display about the local
salmon industry – an interesting diversion
and place to cool off during the summer.

If arriving by bus, alight at the post
office and continue north, following the
signs for the heritage centre. Just after the
icehouse, turn towards the river basin (a
right turn if coming from the car park).
Pass the sailing boats on your right as you
approach the water, then bear right
towards the windsock, passing the
boatyard and an excellent café with
outside tables.

As you follow the curve of the bay, you

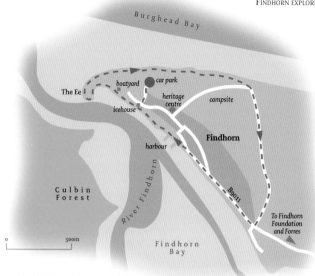

Burghead Bay

The Ee

boatyard

car park

heritage centre

icehouse

campsite

Findhorn

harbour

River Findhorn

Culbin Forest

Bg012

To Findhorn Foundation and Forres

Findhorn Bay

0   500m

are on the shingle spit known as the Ee. Formed by waves bringing sand and pebbles across the bay and almost cutting off the river from the sea, it has created the natural harbour and haven for wildlife of Findhorn Bay and its shape changes constantly. Take care rounding the end of the spit as there is deep water and strong currents near the shore. Across the water, the pines and dunes of Culbin Forest can look almost tropical on a sunny day.

Soon the freshwater meets the salty sea and the route continues along the sand and pebbly beach to the right. Keep an eye out for dolphins and and seals as you walk east to the sixth set of wooden steps. These lead to the East Dunes car park where anti-tank traps from World War II can be seen. Bear left to take the road

inland, crossing the dunes. At the houses, keep straight ahead to the main road. Here, you can detour left to the Findhorn Foundation. The Foundation is many things to many people, but has at its heart a 'new age' spiritual community and eco-village (as well as a great café). Visitors are welcome and there is a small visitor centre where guided tours are offered.

Otherwise, turn right to follow the road along the river to the village. At the war memorial, either continue beside the water or take the road inland which passes pretty cottages to reach the shop and Bakehouse Café. Carry on to the north end of the village to return to the West Dunes car park at the start.

◀ Upturned boats at Findhorn Harbour

Roseisle forest and dunes

Distance 3.5km **Time** 1 hour 30
Terrain easy, waymarked paths through
forest and dunes **Map** OS Explorer 423
Access nearest bus stops at College of
Roseisle, 4km from the start

**Get back to nature with this exploration of
the Roseisle pines, planted to stabilise the
dunes backing one of Moray's finest
beaches. The sands aren't the only family
attraction, with barbeque stands, plenty
of picnic tables and – if you are lucky
enough to spot them – red squirrels.**

Roseisle is reached from the B9089 just
northeast of Forres. Begin by heading west
between the road and the coast on the
white waymarked trail. Soon it reaches an
open viewpoint over the beach with a long
line of concrete blocks – placed in World

War II to halt tank progress in the event of
an invasion – snaking into the distance
towards the wind turbines at Findhorn.
In the other direction, the sands stretch
towards Burghead.

Take the path past the picnic table into
the pines and then across a more open
area. Turn left at a junction to pass an old
war building and accompany a burn
inland. At the track, turn right to cross a
bridge and then immediately left onto a
path alongside a fence. This meandering
path has an air of *Hansel and Gretel* about it
as it wanders through the dense pines, but
instead of a gingerbread house the
building you are looking for is a bird hide,
very useful for spotting the red squirrels
which are common here. To reach the hide,
turn right at the track and then right again

◄ Remains of tank traps on the sands at Roseisle

onto a camouflaged walkway. In addition to hungry squirrels, the feeders attract a variety of woodland birds and you can also amuse yourself reading the jottings in the visitors' book of those simply seeking shelter in bad weather with never a bird or squirrel to be seen.

Return to the track from the hide and turn left. Very soon a white-marked path leads to the right into the forest. The dunes adjacent to the sea are reached and the path bears right through them before crossing a bridge to return to the track. Turn left and immediately after the bridge branch right to follow red marker posts for the return stretch. Keep your eyes peeled for a path on the left which is easily missed, and follow this until it reaches a wider path, then bear right on the sandy trod which leads back to the car park.

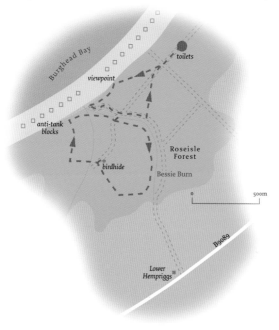

Burghead Bay

Distance 5.5km **Time** 1 hour 30
Terrain good waymarked paths and
sandy beach **Map** OS Explorer 423
Access regular bus from Elgin
to Burghead

**Starting from the fishing village of
Burghead, the families enjoying the fine
sands are soon left behind as you skirt
along the vast crescent of beach towards
Findhorn before returning through the
pines and dunes of Roseisle Forest. Allow
plenty of time to dawdle on the beach or
amongst the dunes, sunbathing or
watching for dolphins.**

Burghead is a typical Moray Firth
fishing village, pretty on a warm sunny
day but dour and forbidding in a winter
storm. It is the scene of the annual
burning of the Clavie on the original New
Year's Day when a barrel full of burning
tar and wood is held aloft on a pole by
members of the Clavie crew, made up of
local fishermen, and paraded past the
fishing boats before becoming part of a
larger fire on the hilltop. This pagan
festival probably dates back to the 1600s,
and it is said that the ashes from the
Clavie bring good luck and ward off
witchcraft. The town is well worth a look
around, especially the harbour area,
Pictish fort, visitor centre and impressive
chambered well, all of which are signed
from the harbour.

This walk starts near the southern end
of Burghead off the B9089 at the entrance
to Burghead Sands Holiday Park, where
there is a car park. From here, follow the

◄ Looking to Burghead from the beach

lane down to the beach and head left across the fine sands. The magnificent curving bay stretches all the way to Findhorn – a tempting objective if transport can be arranged.

In summer, the first part of the beach is popular with holidaying families, but soon any crowds are left behind and you are likely to have as large and empty a stretch of sand as you could wish for. There is a chance of sighting the famous Moray Firth dolphins, although they do not perform on demand and are only likely to put in an appearance after you've given up looking. After 2km, look out for a small burn flowing out across the sand – this is not always visible lower down the beach so look towards the dunes. Before the burn, take a path inland, passing a set of huge concrete blocks, part of the World War II defences against a land invasion.

The path curves back past a stone-built ruin, wrongly marked as a public convenience on some maps. Take the left-hand fork here; the path soon enters the pine forest and eventually reaches a track. Following the sign for Burghead, turn left both here and again at the next junction. At a further junction, continue straight ahead along a path built by prisoners of

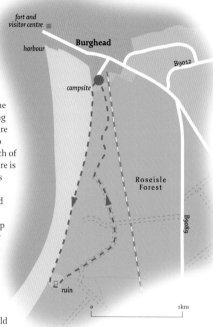

war, interned in a nearby camp and known as the Burma Road. The path winds pleasantly through the pine-covered dunes before reaching a children's play area just outside the caravan park. Go through the gate and follow the track between the caravans, keeping left at a junction to return to the parking area.

29

Hopeman to Lossiemouth

Distance 9km **Time** 3 hours (one way)
Terrain coast path, rough going in
places and sometimes muddy
Map OS Explorer 423 **Access** regular buses
from Lossiemouth to Elgin and from Elgin
to Burghead via Hopeman for the return

This walk explores an excellent and varied
section of coast, combining sea stacks and
coves with lovely sandy stretches.
Although linear, there is a bus service
linking the end of the route to the start.

Hopeman is a small village built at the
beginning of the 19th century to
accommodate people displaced during the
Highland Clearances. It has a small
harbour situated between two sandy
beaches. A regular bus service runs
between Burghead and Elgin, stopping on
the main road in Hopeman; for a slightly
longer walk, adding around 4km to the
total distance, you could start in nearby
Burghead and follow the Moray Coast Trail
signs from the visitor centre just east of
the harbour.

If starting from Hopeman, make your
way down to the harbour and turn right to
reach East Beach, where there is a car park.
Take the path past the picnic table and
pavilion to skirt behind a very colourful
line of beach huts. Follow the signed
coastal path, ignoring a turn on the right
which leads to the Braemou Well, and keep
left of the golf course. Now the route
begins to climb above high cliffs; keep
right where the path forks unless you want

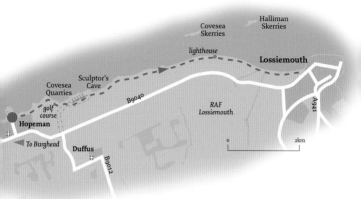

to detour down to the sheltered beach at Clashach Cove. Continuing on the top path, bear left onto a track and then turn off to the right just before the entrance to Covesea Quarry.

Way before man had appeared on earth, early reptiles, probably the ancestors of the dinosaurs, were living in an ancient dune system on this very spot. The cliffs themselves are composed of the same dune system, compressed and fossilised over millions of years. The fossilised remains of these ancient creatures' footprints have been uncovered by the quarrying, and many of the finds are displayed on the blocks of rock on the right. Follow the path into the high gorse bushes, alive with yellow flowers and the distinctive coconut smell for much of the summer, until a sculpture of a fulmar marks an excellent viewpoint. The cliffs are a popular nesting area for this small gull.

Near the coastguard lookout, go left to rejoin the clifftop, beneath which is Sculptor's Cave containing pictish carvings but not easily accessible from the land due to the cliffs. As the path progresses, it passes a sea stack and there is a view to Covesea Lighthouse in the distance. Carry on above a sandy bay and a second seemingly top-heavy stack with an arch in the base. Further on, the path descends towards a long beach, reaching it between two giant rocks. Unless the tide is very high, at which time the path through the dunes should be taken, the best route is to walk across the expanse of sand, passing beneath the lighthouse and coastal defences. After a further 2km of sand, Lossiemouth is reached, although advance warning is given by the roar of the jets from the nearby air base. Go through West Beach car park and walk along the road into the town, where a regular bus service runs to Elgin and Burghead.

◀ Colourful beach huts at Hopeman

31

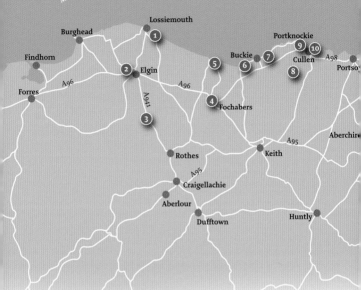

Elgin, capital of Moray, is an interesting mix of ancient and modern – check out the impressive historical ruins of Elgin Cathedral – the Lantern of the North – and nearby Spynie Palace which was the home of its bishops. This former religious centre still has Moray's best shopping and leisure facilities, and easy access to the coast, hills and woods of the region.

Out along the coast itself are the former fishing towns of Lossiemouth and Buckie, now just as busy with leisure boats and personnel from the nearby RAF bases. The beaches in this area are superb, making for ideal walking with good opportunities to spot seals, dolphins and seabirds. The more active-minded can try to catch a wave as surfing and kite-surfing are both popular at Lossiemouth. Further east, the coastline becomes more rugged with some fascinating rock formations en route to the traditional port of Cullen. Home to the delicious Cullen Skink soup, this is also a great place to grab a locally made ice cream or fish supper in the shadow of the old railway viaduct; a perfect end to a great day out in Moray.

The Bow Fiddle Rock near Portknockie ▶

Elgin, Lossiemouth and Buckie

Lossiemouth East Beach

**Distance 6.25km Time 1 hour 30
Terrain** faint path between dunes and
river, woodland track, sand and pebble
beach **Map** OS Explorer 423 **Access** regular
bus from Elgin

**Cross a long and wonderful old wooden
footbridge to reach the East Beach where
surfers tackle the powerful breaking
waves. This circuit follows a tidal section
of the River Lossie before returning along
the sands; a good walk for spotting
seabirds and other wildlife.**

'Lossie', as it is locally known, grew up
as a trading port to serve nearby Elgin and
was once a popular resort on the railway.
Nowadays its sandy beaches and golf
courses (including one designed by the
legendary Old Tom Morris) still attract
visitors and the resident population is
swelled by the RAF base here. If driving,
park at the East Beach car park next to the
narrow Spynie Canal, built by Thomas

Telford as a flood alleviation scheme.
Cross the bridge over the canal to reach
the edge of Seatown. More than 50 low-
roofed cottages are huddled into this
small area and were traditionally occupied
by fishermen. The impressive wooden
footbridge spans the River Lossie, linking
the town to the expansive East Beach, and
was built to encourage daytrippers
coming off the Moray Coast Railway to
spend more time here. Today, the beach is
popular with families and attracts a band
of kite-surfers and regular surfers drawn
by the quality of the breaking waves.

Cross the bridge to reach the strip of
dunes with the East Beach on the far side.
Don't pass through the dunes but turn
right, following a faint path upriver along
the tidal section of the River Lossie.
Depending on the state of the tide, it is
sometimes necessary to skirt round
muddy sections, but it is usually possible
to stay fairly near to the riverside, keeping

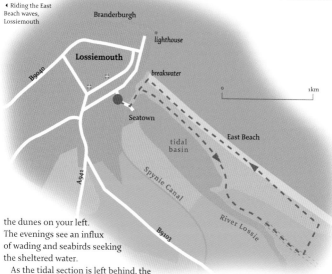

◀ Riding the East Beach waves, Lossiemouth

Branderburgh

Lossiemouth

lighthouse

B9040

breakwater

0 ———————— 1km

Seatown

tidal basin

East Beach

A941

Spynie Canal

River Lossie

B9103

the dunes on your left. The evenings see an influx of wading and seabirds seeking the sheltered water.

As the tidal section is left behind, the route shadows the riverside itself, eventually heading into the pinewoods on a track. At a junction, bear left on a bigger track, then keep an eye out for a wide sandy path rising over the dunes to the left. Take this to climb two sets of dunes before reaching the beach. Now turn left to follow the shore back towards Lossiemouth. Behind you, Spey Bay stretches all the way to Buckie with the prominent dome of the Bin of Cullen seen against the skyline. Soon enough, the pebbly shore gives way to fine sand which gives a lovely walking surface all the way back to the start of the East Beach. Although the dunes near the town look completely natural they are, in fact, man-made. Disused railway carriages from the

Moray Coastal Line were placed on the beach to encourage a barrier of sand to form, protecting Seatown from rough seas which now pound the dunes and breakwater.

Turn left through a gap in those dunes to return to the footbridge and cross this back to the start. Any low-flying aircraft roaring overhead is likely to be from RAF Lossiemouth. As well as a Search and Rescue helicopter function, the base is host to a number of air squadrons, including 617 Squadron, famous for its role in the May 1943 'Dambusters' bombing raid on the dams above Germany's industrial heartland of the Ruhr Valley.

35

River Lossie and Quarrelwood

Distance 9.5km **Time** 3 hours (round trip)
Terrain roads with pavement, shared
cycleway, riverside and woodland paths
Map OS Explorer 423 **Access** regular bus
and train services to Elgin on the
Inverness-Aberdeen route

This exploration of the historic city of
Elgin starts from the cathedral and
follows the river to reach Quarrelwood,
source of the cathedral stone. From here,
the walk can be extended along a choice of
waymarked routes. The walk time given
is for the complete round trip, but this
could be halved by taking a bus back to
the city centre.

Elgin Cathedral is an imposing structure
even in its ruined state; it dates back to
the 13th century. There is some on-street
parking here, and the railway station and
city centre car parks are nearby. For a long
time, the cathedral served as the spiritual
heart of Moray until the Protestant
Reformation of 1560. Known as the
Lantern of the North, the yellow-
sandstone building could be seen for
miles across the relatively flat
surroundings. If you have time, it is well
worth visiting Spynie Palace – once the
fortified home of the Bishops, which is
around 2km north of Elgin by road.

To begin the walk, turn down King
Street, passing the entrance to the Biblical
Garden on the left, and cross the
pedestrian bridge over the River Lossie.
Take the first left onto Kingsmills Court
and turn left again next to a warehouse
and then go straight on to join a
cyclepath. This follows the banks of the

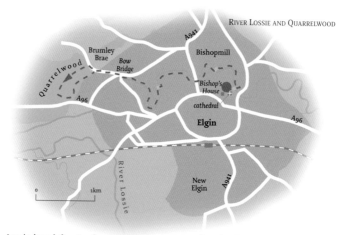

Lossie; keep left onto a larger path and then take the next left to cross a bridge back over the river. At the park, bear right to follow the route next to the river and then pass the boating lake on the left to climb up to another bridge. Do not cross this but, instead, continue ahead under a roadbridge to carry on alongside the river on the cyclepath, passing the home of Elgin City Football Club.

Once past the leisure centre, turn right to cross a metal bridge and keep left along the riverside path through the trees. This skirts a playing field and passes the High School. After a small climb through the trees, the path branches: keep left here and then right at the next fork to stay on the wider path, above the river. At a third fork, branch left to soon reach Morriston Road, and head across this onto Brumley Brae directly opposite. Follow this uphill, looking out for a path into the woods on the left.

When you reach a fencepost, turn left onto a broad path amongst gnarled but magnificent oak trees. After a while, turn right up wooden steps to reach the Quarrelstone. This commemorates the use of stone from this area for local building for centuries. There is a map with routes through the forest here which can be used to extend the walk if required. Otherwise, take the shorter loop described here which passes through some of the best woodland. Continue on the path to the left of the Quarrelstone and soon take a right-hand path uphill to Brumley Brae car park. Follow the tarmac path to the left and carry on along this through a clearing, ignoring any turnings to stay on the main path. At a crossroads, drop left downhill to soon join a wider path, bearing left through impressive trees to return to Brumley Brae. From here, you can retrace the outward route to the centre of Elgin via the cycleway signs or alternatively catch a bus from the stop on Morriston Road.

Millbuies Country Park

Distance **2.7km** Time **45 minutes**
Terrain **easy, clear paths, some steps; care
should be taken with small children near
the water; the park is open from 8.30am
till dusk** Map **OS Explorer 423** Access **bus
from Elgin and Dufftown stops at
Fogwatt on the A941, a short distance
from the park entrance**

**Delve into an oasis of green foliage and
perfect reflections at this country park
just 7km from Elgin. Boats can be hired
with permits for trout fishing, but most
visitors enjoy a ramble through the
mixed trees and a spot of birdwatching.**

Millbuies Country Park is a popular
recreation spot just south of Elgin and
makes a pleasant stop for a short walk.
There are picnic facilities and plenty of
room for a family kick-about near the car
park. To start the walk, take the path

behind the information board, soon
entering a thick tunnel of rhododendrons.

After crossing a small bridge, the route
leads down through tall trees to reach the
shore of the loch. This was created as a
fishing loch by a former landowner who
dammed several local burns. The whole
area was later acquired by local
businessman, George Boyd Anderson, in
the 1930s who used the sheltered position
and fertile soils to begin growing a variety
of exotic trees and shrubs. In 1956, the
estate was gifted to the City of Elgin and
the development and opening up of
access to the public was largely down to
the efforts of one councillor, George
Edgar. He spent many weekends digging
ditches and making footpaths at the site
to enable public access, and also added to
the plantings. A cairn in his memory can
be seen to the left of the path.

◀ Millbuies Loch

Do not cross the dam but instead carry on along the path, soon reaching a hut where you can hire fishing boats. Shortly, the bridge dividing the two lochs comes into view. This was originally part of the Deanshaugh Bridge which spanned the River Lossie in the centre of Elgin, transported here when the city's bridge was replaced in the early 1960s.

Cross it and turn right on the far shore to follow the path through tall pine trees, home to red squirrels that may be seen or heard scuttling up and down the trunks with amazing ease. At the far end of the loch, steps lead down to the dam and you then cross the outflow to stay on the lower path by the water's edge. The higher path provides a slightly longer alternative route which rises through the trees. Pass the wooded isle and a shelter which is a good spot for birdwatching. Turn right before the bench to cross the middle bridge once more and then left on the far side.

As the path climbs through pines, keep left at a fork to soon reach a bridge and the first dam. Cross this and bear right to return through the rhododendron tunnel to the parking area.

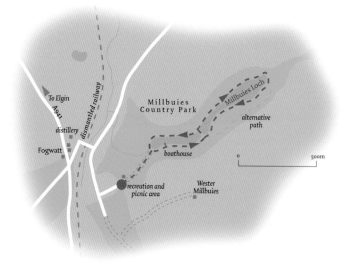

39

The Winding Walks and Peep's View

Distance 3km **Time** 1 hour
Terrain clear, waymarked paths, lots of
short up and down sections; alternative
route on wider tracks is suitable for some
all-terrain buggies **Map** OS Explorer 424
Access regular buses from Elgin and
Huntly on the Inverness-Aberdeen route
and from Buckie

**This peaceful forestry walk travels uphill
by a gushing burn before returning via
Peep's View, where a Victorian wooden
gazebo enjoys a splendid outlook over
the Moray coastal plains.**

Fochabers is a large village on the banks
of the Spey, now best known as the home
of Baxters soups and jams. The firm
started life here as a small grocery store
and now has a large factory and visitor
centre on the edge of the village. The
Winding Walks car park (parking charge)
is a little east of Fochabers on the A98 to

Buckie. Begin by taking the track on the
far right of the car park as you face the
information board, almost immediately
turning left onto a red waymarked path
which rises uphill.

The entire area around Fochabers was
once dominated by the Gordon Estate
which traditionally provided employment
for most of the residents. In the 19th
century, the Duke of Gordon, a keen
forester, built a number of the paths and
bridges in these woods, which formed
part of his extended garden at nearby
Gordon Castle.

At the sign for the Winding Paths, you
can choose between the smaller, more
intimate and rugged path which weaves
between the trees close to the Small Burn
or the wider path which is waymarked in
red. Both meet up again where the walk
crosses the burn. If staying on the larger
path, carry straight on where a path goes

◄ Twisted pine, Leitch's Wood

off to the left at a bench. Both routes climb steadily through a mixture of pines, including western red cedar and spruce and the noble fir, now more commonly seen as small Christmas trees rather than the fully mature specimens here. The winding walk emerges near a wooden bridge; cross this and pass the picnic table to reach a wide track, where you turn right. The red trail brings you to this track just slightly higher up; turn right to reach the meeting point. Almost immediately, you branch left onto a smaller path, waymarked in yellow. Younger pines grow here through a thick carpet of blaeberry and heather. At a track, bear right to reach Peep's View. This lovely wooden gazebo, built by the Duke of Gordon, surveys the countryside surrounding Fochabers and makes a great place for a break.

Continue past the gazebo and cross the track to pick up the winding path, this time heading downstream. At the bottom of a flight of steps, turn left, soon taking the right-hand fork to descend more steps and reach a wider path. Turn right here (or you can detour to a small pond ahead) to shortly reach the car park.

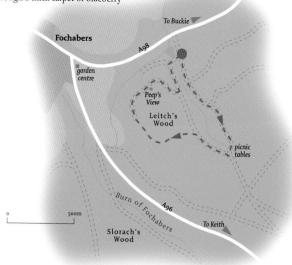

Fochabers

To Buckie

A98

garden centre

Peep's View

Leitch's Wood

picnic tables

Burn of Fochabers

A96

To Keith

0   500m

Slorach's Wood

Spey Bay circuit

Distance 6.5km **Time** 2 hours
Terrain narrow paths which can be very wet underfoot in winter, pebble and sand shoreline, minor road; care needed on crossing the golf course
Map OS Explorer 424 **Access** daily bus from Fochabers (school times only)

Combine a visit to the wildlife centre with a circular walk through woodland and across the golf course, before returning along the beach. Keep an eye out for dolphins and seabirds.

At the far end of Spey Bay there is a car park. The Whale and Dolphin Conservation Society run a wildlife centre here (Apr–end Oct) which is well worth a visit to know what to look out for on the walk. The adjacent Tugnet Ice House is also interesting; it was used to store ice to pack salmon landed here before it was sent to market in London.

To start, walk inland back along the road, passing several houses. Just after the bend by the Spey Bay Hotel, look out for a tall concrete building and turn left here, following the thistle logo of the Speyside Way. Almost immediately, branch right onto a path which accompanies a fence. There is a dip which is sometimes flooded in winter, although usually passable with care. Once in the woods, keep to the Speyside Way markers, staying left where a path leaves towards the road on the

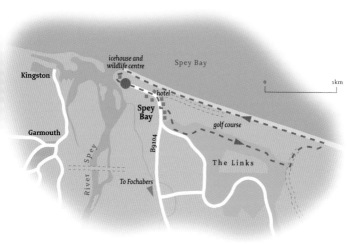

Kingston

icehouse and wildlife centre

Spey Bay

0   1km

hotel

Spey Bay

golf course

Garmouth

River Spey

B9104

The Links

To Fochabers

right. This area is also prone to winter flooding, but signed diversions are usually put in place on any particularly bad stretches. After a straight section along a wide break in the pine trees, the route emerges onto a farm track.

The Speyside Way continues inland towards Buckie from here, so leave it and turn left. Go through a gateway and cross the golf course on a well-worn route leading diagonally to the right. You should look out for any golfers and try not to disturb them – wait until they have played their shots. Aim for the fence near the top of the pebble embankment, and then head down the shingle to reach the beach.

Turn left for the delightful beach stroll back to Spey Bay. Unless the tide is very

high, it is possible to walk along the sand. Behind you, the prominent hill is the Bin of Cullen east of Buckie. Beyond the surf, you may be lucky enough to catch a glimpse of the Moray Firth dolphins or an inquisitive seal; more likely you will be accompanied by the many waders that dart back and forth along the edge of the waves in search of tasty morsels brought up by the water.

As the buildings at Spey Bay draw close, you could make your way directly up to the road. However, it is worth venturing across the pebbly spit to the point where the River Spey meets the sea to watch the swirling waters. From here, aim straight for the three turf roofs of the icehouse to reach the car park.

◀ *Endless surf and shingle, Spey Bay*

Buckie and Portgordon

Distance 8.25km **Time** 2 hours 30
Terrain waymarked paths, tracks and
roads with pavements, some sections
of main road **Map** OS Explorer 424
Access regular bus from Fochabers
and Banff

From the fishing port of Buckie, follow the
coast to neighbouring Portgordon before
returning on the remains of the disused
Moray Coast Railway.

Buckie grew up as a thriving fishing and
shipbuilding port, halfway between the
important centres of Elgin and Banff.
Whilst these traditional industries have
suffered the same decline as elsewhere,
both do still survive with some fish and
shellfish processing and exporting firms,
whilst shipbuilding skills are used to
repair and refit lifeboats and MOD vessels.

If arriving by car, there is parking at Cluny
Square in the centre of Buckie. This walk
is signed as the Gollachy Circuit. From the
Square, take the road that descends north
towards the sea, passing the large war
memorial. Turn left, as signed for
Portgordon, but then branch right after
the corner to avoid the main road. This
leads you through The Yardie, a jumble
of old fishermen's houses with drying
greens and clothes lines facing the sea.
Keep left along the lane to return to the
main road and turn right.

After the road crosses the Buckie Burn,
keep right at a fork and pass the start of
the Speyside Way. This long-distance
route extends inland to Aviemore in the
Cairngorms. Follow the path, which bears
right and passes a number of houses
close to the sea. After heading between

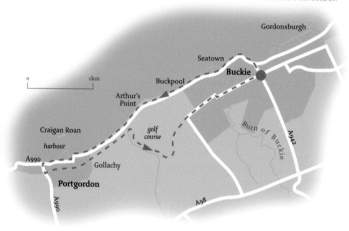

two white posts, keep an eye out for the thistle logo of the Speyside Way and turn left when indicated to briefly rejoin the main road for a short distance before branching right to skirt behind the next set of houses. The path crosses a track, passing a ruined house as it continues along the coast. A quick section of main road is needed to get past a single house before the path goes off once more on the right. The rocky shoreline here is a good place to spot both grey and common seals. The greys can be identified by their longer Roman noses whilst the commons have a more dog-like head shape. Both are inquisitive and will bob in the water like bottles to take a good look at any passing walkers. At another derelict building, take the track which passes to the right of the first houses of Portgordon.

Turn right at a T-junction and then left at the harbour where a few fishing boats

are still moored. Follow the seafront and then turn left along the main road to head inland (SP Keith and Fochabers). After a short rise, turn left along the cycle route and follow the old Moray Coast Railway (SP Buckie). The railway ran until 1968 and was popular with daytrippers who would visit the beaches, outdoor swimming pool and golf courses. It now forms a cyclepath which can be followed most of the way along the clifftops to Cullen. Our route, however, turns off after crossing a bridge over the Burn of Gollachy; bear right here to climb uphill, branching right again at the next junction. Carry on along the edge of the golf course until you meet a road. Turn left here and continue ahead at the next junction on the edge of Buckie, aiming for a prominent church. Pass to the right of the church to continue, crossing the Buckie Burn and eventually returning to Cluny Square.

◀ Old railway line near Portgordon

Strathlene Sands to Portknockie

Distance 5.5km **Time** 2 hours (one way)
Terrain coastal path with unprotected
cliffs and steep steps in places, shared
cycleway **Map** OS Explorer 425
Access regular bus can be caught for
return from Portknockie

This short and varied section of
the Moray coast links the fishing
communities of Findochty and
Portknockie. Catch the regular bus
back to the start or make a day of it by
walking the return.

Start from the car park at Strathlene
Sands just to the east of Buckie along the
A942. (If you start from Buckie instead,
follow Commercial Road along the back
of the fishing boat-filled harbour to pass
shipbuilding yards and then walk by the
A942 through Portessie to reach

Strathlene Sands.) Head through the car
park and over the springy turf behind the
sands to join the driveway leading to the
old Strathlene House Hotel. A reminder of
the area's popularity as a coastal resort
during the 1930s and 40s when the railway
would bring daytrippers to the station at
Portessie, the hotel even had its own
seawater swimming pool, the remains of
which can be seen on the shore.

Continue ahead when the surfaced path
ends onto rougher ground along the
rocky foreshore. Steps soon lead to the
clifftop golf course. Take care not to
disturb play and keep to the left edge of
the course for a very short distance before
another flight of steps leads down to the
continuation of the coast path. This route
forms part of the Moray Coast Trail, a
72km long-distance walking route

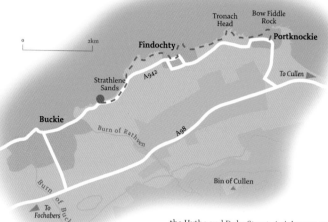

stretching from Forres to Cullen. The Moray Way has been designed to join part of this coast trail with a section of the Speyside Way and the Dava way at Grantown-on-Spey to make a satisfying circular route taking about a week.

As the outskirts of Findochty are reached, cross a rocky inlet on a bridge and keep straight ahead to pass the caravan park to arrive at the attractive harbour. The traditional white fishing cottages here hark back to the village's past as a thriving whitefish port. Now most of the boats in the harbour and marina are leisure vessels.

Findochty has a shop and a couple of pubs for refreshment. Follow the road around the back of the harbour and keep an eye out for the cycleway signs which lead you onto Storlochy Street,

the Hythe and Duke Street. A right turn at the end of Duke Street leads to the beach at Sandy Creek. Cross the back of the sands and climb up the steep cliff path to join the well-surfaced shared cycleway. Bear left along it to pass the cemetery and enjoy the views over the rocky coastline of Tronach Head which the route now passes.

Eventually the path reaches Cliff Terrace on the edge of Portknockie. Keep straight ahead, with the harbour visible down on the left. To reach the bus stop for the return journey, turn right up Harbour Place and right again to reach Church Street, where the bus stops outside the small supermarket. Alternatively, the outward route can be reversed and different views enjoyed on the walk back. This can be shortened by taking the signed inland cycleway from Findochty which follows the route of the old railway.

◀ Findochty Harbour

The Bin of Cullen

Distance **5.5km** Time **1 hour 30**
Terrain **clear forest and moorland tracks**
Map **OS Explorer 425** Access **no public transport to start**

The wide coastal strip south of the Moray Firth is mostly low-lying, making the several small, rounded hills more prominent. The Bin of Cullen is the best of these, with an easy ascent and fine views.

Although the Bin can be climbed from Portknockie, the most straightforward route starts via a woodland accessed from the B9018. To reach the start from Cullen by car, follow the A98 eastwards, taking the first right on the edge of the village onto the B9018. After 3km, turn right (signed Hill of Maud) onto a minor road. Around 2km further on, the road bends left and a track leads right, with limited parking at this entrance: take care not to obstruct the access.

Enter the forestry by the track, keeping straight ahead when it splits. After crossing a small bridge, turn left at a junction to climb uphill, passing some fine Scots pines. The track levels off at the bealach between the Bin and its smaller cousin, Little Bin, although the trees obscure the view of this. Turn left here for

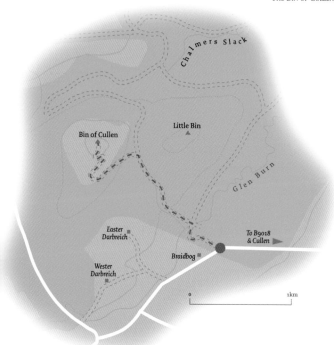

a gradual ascent across the southern side of the larger 'Bin' (a corruption of the Gaelic *Beinn*). Keep on the main track when it starts to zigzag more steeply, ignoring the shortcut which is used by mountain bikers often descending at terrifying speed.

The track climbs clear of the trees to reveal impressive views inland, with the domed outline of Knock Hill prominent to the southeast. The stony track soon curves around to reach the summit of the

Bin of Cullen, offering a grand sweep along the Moray coastline. A view indicator identifies the various peaks and landmarks. On a clear day, the pyramidal shape of Morven in Caithness can be made out across the water, and the view takes in much of the Moray Firth as well as the distant Cairngorms in the opposite direction. Nearby, the village of Cullen is well seen, looking down on its disused railway viaducts. The descent is best made by retracing your steps.

◀ Looking north from the Bin of Cullen

Cullen Bay and Portknockie

Distance 7.5km **Time** 2 hours 30
Terrain mostly good paths; rocky section
on shore may be impassable at very high
tide **Map** OS Explorer 425 **Access** regular
bus from Buckie and Banff on the
Inverness-Aberdeen route

Explore one of the most scenic sections
of the Moray coast on this circular walk.
Cross the sands of Cullen Bay to see
the spectacular rock formations of the
Whale's Mouth and the Bow Fiddle Rock
before reaching Portknockie and
returning inland on the old railway line,
with extensive views.

Famous for Cullen Skink – a delicious
haddock and potato soup – Cullen is a
place of two distinct parts divided by a
steep hill. Start from The Square in the
upper part, opposite the tourist
information centre. Walk down the main
street towards the tightly-packed houses
of Seatown. This is where the fishing
families would have lived, with the richer
merchants and other residents occupying
the larger houses in the upper town. Pass
under the massive railway viaduct and
keep straight ahead to reach the harbour.
Turn left here to pass the Seatown
cottages, staying beside the sea, and cross
a footbridge into a car park and then onto
Cullen Sands. This sweeping sandy bay is

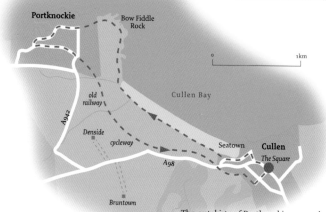

Over Cullen's rooftops to Cullen Bay

divided by two large sea stacks, jutting out of the sand like giant shark fins. Continue to the far end of the sands and follow the rocky ground at the base of the cliffs; this may be impossible at high tide.

After the first small headland, a grassy path makes the going easier just above the high tide line. Pass Jenny's Well and climb atop a section of built-up concrete path, after which a grassy section precedes a diagonal climb to the clifftop.

Look right to see the yawning Whale's Mouth – a deep gash-like natural arch in the cliffs. At the top, a bench provides a resting point with a great view back over Cullen. Bear right along the path that teeters along the steep cliff edge to reach the Bow Fiddle rock. One large sea stack forms the fiddle, while a small stack joined by an arch provides the fiddle, although this image requires some imagination; whatever you decide, it is a striking sight.

The outskirts of Portknockie are reached at some workshops. Take the lane behind these to follow a residential road with good views down to more bizarre-shaped rocks to the right. The road bends left above the harbour; continue to the dead-end sign and turn left towards the main road through Portknockie. Follow this to the left, passing the war memorial and then branching left to walk behind a bus shelter and join the signed cycleway running along the disused railway line.

The line once provided a link along the coast between Portsoy and Lossiemouth and was known as the Moray Coast Railway. This section passes through some cuttings at first, but then has great views over the golf course to Cullen before passing over the dramatic viaduct with the cottages of Seatown seen in miniature far below. Leave the railway at a blue cycle sign and turn right up the street. Take the next left and follow this road back to The Square at the centre of Cullen.

Findlater Castle from Sandend

Distance 5km **Time** 2 hours
Terrain undulating coastal path, can be
a little overgrown in summer, country
lanes **Map** OS Explorer 425
Access bus from Cullen and Banff
on the Inverness-Aberdeen route

Visit Findlater Castle, dramatically
perched above the sea, and the beehive-
shaped Findlater Doocot on this scenic
coastal circular. Return along quiet
country lanes, leaving time to enjoy
the fine beach at Sandend.

There is a parking area near the caravan
park at Sandend, just inland from the
beach. From here, walk along the road
towards the sea, passing a fish smokery.

Look out for a lane signed as the 'Coast
Path to Sunnyside Beach', climb behind
a house and then head right on the path.
From here, the rooftops of the tightly
clustered old fishermen's cottages can be
seen, making the most of the limited
space near the harbour. Cross one stile
and then another to follow the grassy
clifftop path, alternating between the
seaward and landward side of a fence.

Soon the ruins of Findlater Castle are
seen ahead. Teetering on the side of a
15m-high cliff, the castle is built out on a
tiny headland, meaning access is only via
a narrow strip of land. The first records of
the castle relate to preparations for the
Viking invasion by King Haakon in the

1260s. King Alexander III's military efforts to repel the invasion were inadequate and the Vikings ended up occupying the castle for some time. The present-day ruins probably date from the late 14th century and were built by Sir John Sinclair and modelled on Rosslyn Castle just outside Edinburgh, the stronghold of the Sinclair family. The path down to the castle is narrow and unstable, so it may be best to admire it from the viewpoint on the coastal path.

If time allows, a short but steep detour is possible to the lovely sandy cove at Sunnyside, further along the coast. Carry on along the coast path to reach it, though unless you intend to walk onwards to Cullen, you will have to return to this spot. The circular walk continues inland from behind the information board at the castle.

As you cross the fields, the huge white doocot – Scots for dovecote – is well worth the short detour along a path on the right. The doocot dates back to the 16th century and was used to breed pigeons and doves; peering in from the entrance reveals more than 700 nestboxes arranged in tiers on the inside walls. The vast accumulations of droppings were collected and used to fertilise the fields, whilst the young birds or 'peezers' were killed for their meat, squab, which was popular in stews and pies.

Continue along the main path to the ruinous Barnyards of Findlater and through a parking area onto the lane. This soon bears left and then right, before reaching a minor road; turn left and follow this back to Sandend.

◀ Clifftop ruins of Findlater Castle

53

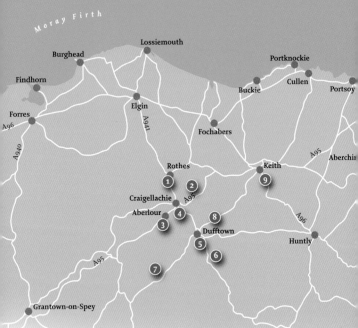

Dufftown is the very heart of Speyside whisky country. The key ingredient – the fresh, clean water from the rolling foothills of the Cairngorms – flows here, whilst the fertile grain-growing coastal plains to the north provide the essential malt. Many of the walks in this area pass distilleries, some offering tours and tastings. The traditional stone buildings of the small towns are complemented by rolling hills, castles and wide fishing rivers.

Ben Rinnes is a great place from which to survey the area, with a vista spreading from the coast to the Cairngorms. As the

highest hill in the area, the walk can be challenging, especially in 'robust' weather, but there are any number of easier routes in sheltered glens, to waterfalls and around lochs. Thrill seekers can try out the mountain bike trails on Ben Aigan, whilst those wanting a more sedate option can poke about the interesting shops and cafés in Aberlour, home to the well-known single malt, as well as Walkers Shortbread. The great River Spey is a legend amongst fly-fishermen, who can be seen standing deep in the water for hours at a time trying to tempt the elusive salmon.

54

Aberlour Square ▶

Dufftown and Keith

The Dounie from Rothes

Distance 5km Time 1 hour 30
Terrain waymarked paths and tracks
Map OS Explorer 424 Access bus from
Forres and Dufftown to Rothes

This short ramble through the Speyside countryside features a whisky distillery, a ruined castle, and a golf course – leaving plenty of time for a round and a dram.

Rothes is a small town situated in the heart of whisky country, on the banks of the Spey. There is parking near the post office in the centre, just off the main A941. From here, return to and cross the main road, turning right and then left into Burnside Street to reach The Glenrothes Distillery. Whisky has been flowing here since 28 December 1879, a day more often remembered for the Tay Bridge Disaster.

From such an inauspicious date, The Glenrothes has gone on to contribute to many well-known blended brands, as well as more recently producing a single malt. Like many Speyside distilleries, Glenrothes' history has been chequered, with American prohibition and a disastrous fire which destroyed more than 20,000 barrels in 1922 being followed by the Great Depression when production reached a low ebb and the distillery closed down for a time.

Walk straight on between the distillery buildings, turning left to cross a footbridge signed for the Dounie Footpath. A delightful section of path accompanies a wooded burn through meadows and into the Muckle Dounie, the larger of the two glens.

The path meanders near the burn until

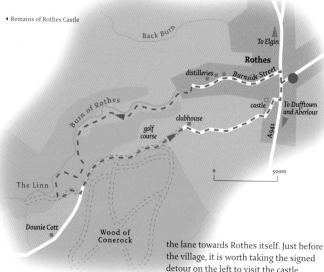

◀ Remains of Rothes Castle

a left turn at a sign for Dounie and Fairies' Well plunges into a plantation. The well is one of the water sources for the distillery and is protected by a manhole cover. The path now continues through the Little Dounie, the second, very narrow and more intimate wooded glen. After a few short flights of steps, a signpost is reached; to the right is a view over the waterfall of The Linn, whilst the walk continues to the left. When the path reaches a track, go left again to reach a T-junction where you turn left. Keep straight ahead to walk alongside Rothes Golf Course, eventually reaching the clubhouse where you follow

the lane towards Rothes itself. Just before the village, it is worth taking the signed detour on the left to visit the castle. Although only one wall remains of the early 13th-century structure, the sheer scale and bulk of this surviving wall gives an impression of the massive dimensions of the fortress. Built on the command of King William of Lion by an aristocrat, Petrus de Pollock, to spread the king's influence and reduce lawlessness, the castle guarded an important transport route in the Middle Ages.

After visiting the castle, return to the lane and carry on downhill, passing the distillery to reach the main road. Take this to the left as far as the church with the clocktower, and turn right here to reach the start point.

Ben Aigan

Distance 8km **Time** 2 hours 30
Terrain straightforward forest tracks and
paths, one very boggy section and rough
path over open moorland near the
summit **Map** OS Explorer 424
Access no public transport to start

With its bald head emerging from the
dense growth of forestry, the summit of
Ben Aigan makes for a great family hill
walk. Although relatively short there is a
proper mountain 'feel' at the top, with
sweeping views across the Moray and
Aberdeenshire countryside.

Whilst Ben Aigan has become
increasingly popular with mountain
bikers in recent years, with the
development of dedicated trails like Pink
Fluffy Bunny and The Hammer, there is

still room for walkers on this delightful
hill. The walk through the pine forests is
rewarded by the expansive moorland
summit with wide-ranging views over
most of Moray.

This ascent route starts from the bike
trail car park, signed off the main A95
between Craigellachie and Keith. Follow
the track west from the car park. This is
the start point for all of the trails, so keep
an eye out for speeding, mud-splattered
cyclists. Once through a gate, stay on the
track passing a felled area on the right.
After about 1km, the track curves right
and rises gently with the mast on Knock
More visible ahead.

The point where the ascent route leaves
the main track is unmarked and can be
hard to spot. Another 750m further on,

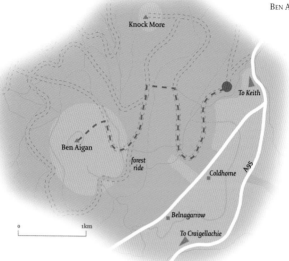

the track bends to the right at a passing space. Just before the bend, leave the track to head up a steep firebreak on the left. A well-worn path tells you that you are on the right route. At a clear crossroads of breaks, keep straight ahead, following a fence on the right; the peaty soil can be very muddy in places. Soon the path emerges onto a track, where you turn left for a more gentle climb. Ignore the bike trails off to the right and then the left as you continue uphill and emerge into open moorland. Here, take the track which bears to the right across the heathery ground.

At another fork, keep left for the short but steep climb to the summit. The top is marked by a rare square trig point at 471m. In hill parlance, Ben Aigan is one of the Marilyns, relatively high hills named

in tongue-in-cheek homage to the Munros which are over 914m. Confusingly, many Scottish Marilyns are also Munros, but not all Munros are Marilyns, as the latter include any hills with a drop of 150m on all sides whereas a Munro just has to attain the fixed height.

The views from the top can take your breath away on a clear day, whilst the wind can do the same on a breezy one. The Moray coastline and Spey Bay are prominent, with the great bulk of Ben Rinnes inland. Walk a short way west to reveal the town of Rothes, its distillery sometimes sending plumes of steam into the air. The way back is by the same outward path and track, remembering to watch out for mountain bikers on the shared sections.

◀ Rothes from the summit of Ben Aigan

Linn of Ruthrie from Aberlour

Distance 3km **Time** 1 hour
Terrain road with pavement, path with
steps; steep drops **Map** OS Explorer 424
Access bus from Elgin, Craigellachie and
Dufftown to Aberlour

**With its lovely riverside park and some
interesting shops and buildings, Aberlour
is a great place in which to potter about.
This leg stretcher climbs above the town
to visit a woodland waterfall before
returning to refuel on the town's famous
shortbread and whisky.**

Buses stop in the main street; otherwise
there is a large signed car park near the
River Spey. To reach this from the central
square, go past the church and under the
old railway. Walk back into town along
this road and, at the square, cross the
main road. Head up Queen's Road

opposite, just to the right of the Co-op,
passing another fine church on the left
along the way.

After passing the hospital on the right,
keep straight ahead at a junction for a
steep uphill climb. Part way up, there is a
useful bench with an excellent view over
the houses. Soon after this, Allachie Drive
leaves to the left; instead of going along
this road, take the path at its start (SP
Fairy Knowe) and climb the steep shortcut
up to the higher road. Continue uphill
along this to the right. It is possible to
make a steep detour up Fairy Knowe,
which is a distinctive and slightly
overgrown knobble topped with standing
stones, just before a large house. Such
cone-shaped hillocks were often thought
to be the home of fairies, and this one has
a great position overlooking Aberlour.

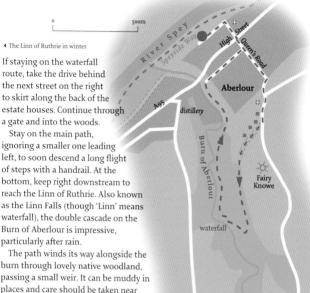

◄ The Linn of Ruthrie in winter

If staying on the waterfall route, take the drive behind the next street on the right to skirt along the back of the estate houses. Continue through a gate and into the woods.

Stay on the main path, ignoring a smaller one leading left, to soon descend a long flight of steps with a handrail. At the bottom, keep right downstream to reach the Linn of Ruthrie. Also known as the Linn Falls (though 'Linn' means waterfall), the double cascade on the Burn of Aberlour is impressive, particularly after rain.

The path winds its way alongside the burn through lovely native woodland, passing a small weir. It can be muddy in places and care should be taken near steep drops to the water. On the far side, Aberlour Distillery comes into view. Half of all Scotland's malt distilleries are located in Speyside, and Aberlour is one of the larger brands. Built on the site of an ancient spring, the distillery has been here since 1879 and now runs tours for visitors keen to see the production process and 'nose' the various strengths of whisky produced.

Stay on the same side of the river, turning right after an electricity substation. This leads to a path beside an old cottage, climbing steps to reach a residential street. Continue past the primary school, then turn left onto Queen's Road to return to the main street. It is well worth checking out some of the individual shops and tearooms, especially the beautiful original interior of the excellent Spey Larder deli, before walking back to the car park. If you have time, the Alice Littler Park by the River Spey is also worth a visit; every summer, it plays host to the popular Aberlour Highland Games where, not surprisingly, bottles of whisky regularly feature as prizes.

Aberlour by the Speyside Way

Distance 12km Time 3 hours (one way)
Terrain fairly level waymarked route,
mainly on old railway lines; muddy and
narrow in places Map OS Explorer 424
Access regular bus between Aberlour
and Dufftown

Follow the Speyside Way past whisky
distilleries and along wooded riverbanks
between the two historic towns of
Dufftown and Aberlour. The return
journey can be made by bus or a linking
hill path, which would add approximately
two hours to the total time.

The four main streets of Dufftown
converge on the attractive clocktower.
Once the town jail, it now houses a tourist
information centre and is the start point
for this walk; there is on-street parking
nearby. Begin by walking down Balvenie
Street (if all the names sound familiar, you
may have seen them on whisky bottles as
Dufftown boasts no less than six
distilleries). At the post office, turn right
into Albert Place and then second left into
Tomnamuidh Road. Take the path next to
the postbox at the bend and follow this as
it curves right into a wood. Bear left at a
fork towards Balvenie Castle. A walk down
the field and around a house brings you to
the impressive ruins, dating back to 1200.

The road leads you downhill around the
grounds; head left at the bottom to pass
Glenfiddich Distillery, another popular
attraction. At the main road, turn right and
then right again just beyond the entrance
to the Keith and Dufftown Railway. Walk
along the remains of the old platform to
the left and then cross a minor road at a
picnic area to continue along the old
railway line. This is an offshoot of the long-
distance Speyside Way and also part of the

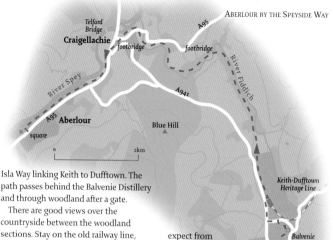

Telford Bridge
Craigellachie
footbridge
A95
footbridge
River Fiddich
River Spey
A95 **Aberlour**
A941
Blue Hill
square
0   2km
Keith-Dufftown
Heritage Line
Balvenie
Castle
Dufftown
clocktower

Isla Way linking Keith to Dufftown. The path passes behind the Balvenie Distillery and through woodland after a gate.

There are good views over the countryside between the woodland sections. Stay on the old railway line, taking care where a couple of landslips have narrowed the path. Eventually, this crosses the River Fiddich, popular with both fly-fishermen and distillers for the peaty but pure water. After crossing the river once more, the path emerges at a park on the edge of the small settlement of Craigellachie. You'll find toilets here, with a shop and two hotels just up the road. If you don't wish to stop, carry on ahead via the sign for Aberlour, now on the official Speyside Way. After a gate, the route runs adjacent to the River Spey, curving through an underpass to run across open farmland. As it nears Aberlour, stay on the path until it comes to a park. Follow the path to the left, aiming for the old station building, which now houses a café and the Speyside Way information centre. Turn left just before the old station to reach the centre of Aberlour. The town has a lovely selection of traditional shops and, as you might

expect from the home of Walkers Shortbread, plenty of tearooms in which to sample the local baking. The bus stop for the return trip to Dufftown can be found on the main street.

For the energetic, there is an alternative walk back over the hills separating the two towns – a map will be needed. To take this route, walk up Queen's Road, turning left onto Allachie Drive shortly after passing the hospital and climbing uphill. Stay on this road as it rises to a junction signed for Dufftown. Continue on a forestry track, following the signs through the trees and then over moorland before the descent through more trees and along a grassy path eventually brings you to a farm track. This leads to Balvenie Road, where a right turn lands you back at the clocktower.

◄ Balvenie Castle

The Giant's Chair

Distance 4.5km Time 1 hour 15
Terrain clear, grassy paths and surfaced
lanes Map OS Explorer 424 Access regular
bus from Aberlour, Craigellachie and
Elgin to Dufftown

**Combine a visit to the historic whisky-
producing village of Dufftown with a
ramble through a wooded gorge to
visit rock formations fit for a giant's
front room.**

The centre of Dufftown is dominated
by the clocktower in the main square.
The walk begins here, and there is on-
street parking both at this site and in the
parking area off Station Road.
From the clocktower, walk south
along Church Street. Ignore the
signed footpaths to the right,
and continue to the junction

opposite Mortlach Church. This was a
separate village before it was absorbed
into Dufftown. The churchyard is worth a
visit to see a Pictish cross, and there is an
earlier symbol stone in the vestibule.
Some parts of the church are ancient,
dating back to 700AD, but most of the
building that can be seen today was
rebuilt at the end of the 19th century.

Follow the sign for the Giant's Chair as
you continue along the road, and go
straight on at the next junction. Dufftown
Distillery, one of six currently operating
around the village, is on the left. Whisky
distilling has long been important to this

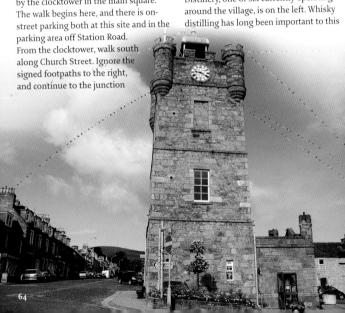

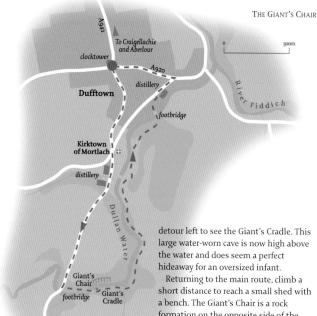

To Craigellachie
and Aberlour

A941

clocktower

A920

distillery

Dufftown

footbridge

**Kirktown
of Mortlach**

distillery

River Fiddich

Dullan Water

Giant's
Chair

footbridge   Giant's
Cradle

0   500m

area, famed for its pure water. There were
once numerous illegal stills and the army
was regularly used to try and rout out the
distillers and smugglers. Dufftown's
economy owes so much to whisky that a
local saying claims that 'if Rome was built
on seven hills, then Dufftown stands on
seven stills'.

Follow the road uphill and past the
warehouses of Pittyvaich Distillery. After
1km, where the road drops downhill, keep
an eye out for a signed path on the left.
This leads you into the wooded glen.
Cross the footbridge over the river and

detour left to see the Giant's Cradle. This
large water-worn cave is now high above
the water and does seem a perfect
hideaway for an oversized infant.

Returning to the main route, climb a
short distance to reach a small shed with
a bench. The Giant's Chair is a rock
formation on the opposite side of the
river. The path takes you on a winding
course, high above the water on the
edge of the steep-sided gorge, before
dropping down to reach the weir where
there is a welcome bench. Dufftown
Distillery can be seen, and sometimes
smelt, on the far side.

At the signpost, a left turn over a
footbridge gives a shortcut back to
Mortlach Church. Otherwise, go straight
on to skirt alongside a cemetery –
ignoring the second bridge. At a fork,
carry straight on and cross the next bridge
to reach Mortlach Distillery. Bear right
along the road to meet the main road, and
then turn left for the clocktower.

◀ Dufftown clocktower

Auchindoun Castle

Distance 2km **Time** 30 minutes
Terrain stony track; just passable for some
all-terrain buggies if a bumpy ride can be
tolerated, uphill section near start; this
crosses grazing land so any dogs should
be on a short lead **Map** OS Explorer 424
Access no public transport to start

What this walk lacks in length, it makes up
for with spades of atmosphere at the
dramatic ruins of Auchindoun Castle,
surrounded by peaceful, semi-wild
scenery. A great spot to visit with children,
but remember to pack the plastic swords.

Auchindoun Castle is located just
southeast of Dufftown. There is limited
parking at the side of the A941 between
Dufftown and Rhynie, just after a bend in
the road and before Raws Cottage if
approaching from the north. Cars are not
allowed up the track towards the castle.
Start the walk up the signed stony track
and continue over a cattle grid. When the
track forks, keep right to pass through a

gate. Once round the corner, aim for the
ruinous farm buildings straight ahead.
The castle can now be seen on the left. At
the end of the fence, bear left across the
field to reach a gate near the castle.
Another inner gate leads through to the
grounds of the castle, imposing even in
their ruined state.

The action-packed history of this
building includes a catalogue of gruesome
and bloody tales. It was originally built in
the 1400s for John, Earl of Mar, but has
been rebuilt a number of times since. John
died in suspicious circumstances in
Edinburgh in 1479 and chroniclers of the
time recorded that he had been murdered
on the word of his own brother, James III,
King of Scotland. The land and castle
were forfeited and presented to one of the
king's favourites, Thomas Cochrane.
A couple of years later, Thomas came to a
sticky end at Lauder Bridge. King James,
accompanied by Cochrane, had assembled
a force to repel the invading English army

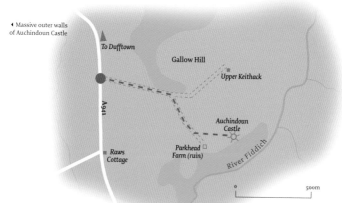

◄ Massive outer walls of Auchindoun Castle

To Dufftown

Gallow Hill

Upper Keithack

A941

Auchindoun Castle

Raws Cottage

Parkhead Farm (ruin)

River Fiddich

0   500m

when they were ambushed by a group of noblemen from Angus in league with the king's other brother, Alexander, Duke of Albany. The king was imprisoned in Edinburgh and Cochrane was hanged from the bridge. Following this, the castle became the stronghold of the Gordons. In 1571, Sir Adam Gordon of Auchindoun became the perpetrator of one of the most notorious deeds in the area's history. He rode to Corgarff Castle to challenge the Forbes of Towie and claim that fortress for the Queen. Forbes was not at home, but his wife, Margaret Campbell, refused his party entry and poured a torrent of abuse at them. A shot fired from the battlements enraged Gordon so much that he torched the castle, burning to death Margaret and 27 family and servants, including a number of children, earning him the nickname, the Herod of the North, and giving rise to a melancholic ballad.

This was not the end of the story, as Auchindoun Castle was burnt down in revenge for the razing of Corgarff Castle. It was rebuilt, but eventually fell into disrepair in the 1800s. Stone was plundered from the site for other local buildings, including Balvenie Castle in Dufftown. In recent times, the castle fell into a dangerous state and public access was restricted. However, a period of restoration by Historic Scotland, completed in 1997, has stabilised the ruins. Today's remains include the walls of an L-shaped towerhouse with cellars. There would have been a massive hall with vaulted ceiling on the first floor and bedrooms on the upper floor.

When you have finished exploring the castle and perhaps enacted your own family feud over a picnic, return along the outward track to the start.

67

Ben Rinnes

Distance 7.5km Time 3 hours 30
Terrain clear hill path; the hill is exposed
and hillwalking gear is needed; winter
skills and equipment are necessary when
under snow Map OS Explorer 424
Access no public transport to start

Moray's classic hill walk and a landmark
from much of the area, Ben Rinnes is one
of the most popular routes in this book.
Eight counties are said to be visible from
the granite summit tor on a clear day.

The most attractive and popular route
up Ben Rinnes is from the parking area at
Glack Harnes on a minor road branching
north from the B9009. Go through the
gate and follow the track which soon
starts to zigzag steadily up the hill. The

views back over Glen Rinnes improve with
every step and can give a useful excuse for
regular breaks.

The path, very obvious in summer, goes
through a gate and continues its upward
climb to the minor rise of Roy's Hill. After
scaling this lump on the side of the Ben,
the path descends slightly with a clear
view of the steeper uphill slog that still
awaits. The area known as the Black Banks
became notoriously eroded a few years
ago as the old path aimed directly up a
very steep slope and became a gully for
rainwater to greatly increase the damage
caused by walkers' boots. However,
sterling work by the Friends of Ben
Rinnes in cooperation with the local
landowners has enabled an excellent new

‹ Well-worn route up Ben Rinnes

zigzag path to be built, easier on the leg muscles as well as the ecology of the hill.

Above the zigzags, the gradient eases and soon the rocky tors near the summit can be seen. Reaching them still requires a bit more effort than an initial upward glance might suggest; however, on a clear day the superb views from the top are a just reward. The trig point juts out from a granite tor and has a useful view indicator with many of the surrounding hills labelled. On a clear day, the eight old counties which are visible are Aberdeenshire, Banffshire, Moray, Nairnshire, Inverness-shire, Ross and Cromarty, Sutherland, and Caithness. Easier to identify and closer to hand is the Moray coast and inland the great plateaux of the Cairngorms. To the east, the distinctive sharp cone of the Mither Tap of Bennachie is prominent. The return is by the same outward route.

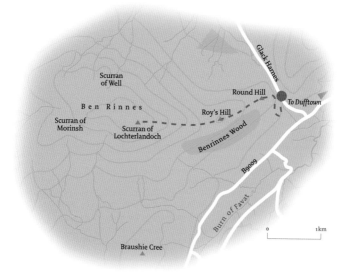

Drummuir Estate

Distance 7.5km Time 2 hours
Terrain waymarked path and track, often
muddy Map OS Explorer 424 Access bus
from Keith stops on B9014 just north of
road to Botriphnie Church; Keith and
Dufftown Railway stops at Drummuir at
weekends (Apr-Sept)

**This ramble around the Drummuir Estate
has great variety, with a loch, forests,
leafy woodland, ponds and fields. The
walk can be combined with a visit to the
castle's former walled garden.**

Drummuir lies south of Keith on the
B9014. The walk starts at Botriphnie
Church just north off the B9014 and a
short way left once over the railway. There
is a parking area here and a board with a
map of the routes. Follow the signed
footpath which crosses a footbridge and
runs alongside the railway. This is the
Keith and Dufftown Railway, an 18km

heritage line and a popular attraction.
The path veers right, crossing back over
the burn, and then runs alongside an old
waterlogged track.

Drummuir Castle can be glimpsed
through the trees up to the right. Now
leased to the whisky and drinks giant,
Diageo, the stately pile was built in 1847 in
the grand Scottish Victorian style. This
period saw a number of large country
estate houses erected in baronial style,
often with turrets and castellated styling.
Drummuir is no exception, with
numerous circular turrets, high chimney
stacks, and an 18m-high lantern tower.
The castle is not generally open to the
public, but the walled garden is soon
reached and can be visited.

Continue on the path, keeping below
the walled garden and passing through
pine trees, over a bridge and straight
ahead to a junction. The track to the right

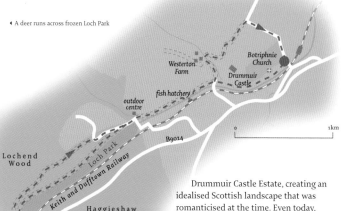

◀ A deer runs across frozen Loch Park

Drummuir Castle Estate, creating an idealised Scottish landscape that was romanticised at the time. Even today, there are lovely views across the water, although the track can be churned and muddy underfoot.

At the far end of the loch, turn right (blue marker) onto an uphill track. Carry straight on until you reach a minor road and then follow this directly ahead down to the Adventure Centre. From here, retrace the outward route to the junction with the Westerton track mentioned earlier. Back at this point, turn left uphill towards Westerton.

signed 'Westerton' is used later in the walk, but for now carry straight on. Turn left across another bridge to follow a loop path round a salmon hatchery, rejoining the track further on. From here, you can either continue on the track or take the newer (but wetter) path which runs just alongside in the trees on the left.

Cross a field and pass between the buildings of the Loch Park Adventure Centre, which provides outdoor activities and watersports as well as rural skills training. After crossing the road, take the lower track (not the one signed Isla Way) near the shores of the loch. The loch was created in Victorian times to enhance the

Pass a house and turn sharp right at a ruined farmhouse. A track leads down to a burn which is crossed on stepping stones; remain on the track, eventually passing an estate cottage. Go straight ahead to reach a minor road and then turn right downhill, passing the gatehouse for Drummuir Castle before taking the next turn on the right to return to the start.

Tarnash Falls and Dunnyduff Wood

Distance 5.5km Time 1 hour 15
Terrain waymarked paths, roads with
pavements, sometimes muddy in the
woods Map OS Explorer 424
Access regular buses from Fochabers
and Huntly to Keith on the Inverness-
Aberdeen route

**Known as the friendly town, Keith has
two parts, each with a square off the
main road to Aberdeen. This pleasant
circuit runs from the centre of town to
explore the nearby woods and waterfall.**

Reidhaven Square is the larger, central
square of Keith and is signed as Keith
Square from the main A96. There is
parking here, as well as the main bus stop.
The town is split into two sections on
either side of the River Isla. This part, on
the east side, was a later addition laid out
by the Earl of Findlater in 1755. The older

part grew up as a popular stopping point
for cattle drovers, although the town's
economy later grew from the textile and
distilling industries – there are still four
distilleries based in Keith. The main street
and shopping area leads off down Mid
Street, to the right as you look up the
Square. This route sets out in the opposite
direction, turning to the left at the central
roundabout. At the end of the road turn
left to reach the A96. Cross this with care
and walk along the road opposite, bearing
right where it forks into Old Den Road.
Just after the last house, a path rises uphill
on the left; take this and keep to the main
path, ignoring any branches off towards
the houses. The path meanders through
lovely mature trees before dropping to
accompany the Den Burn.

At a junction after a short rise, bear
right and go downhill to cross a green

◄ The Den, Keith

bridge, then follow the burn upstream into Dunnyduff Wood. At the next junction, detour to the right to cross another bridge and continue until there are good views of the Tarnash Falls. Return to the junction and this time turn right up the steps into the pine forest. At the top, go left over a bridge and keep straight ahead on a level track. Soon this narrows to a path which can sometimes be muddy. Wind through the woods, crossing a small bridge before emerging at the edge of the woods. The clear path bears right and keeps to the edge of the

trees where there is a viewpoint with a bench overlooking Keith. The prominent dome is St Thomas' Chapel at the top of the Square.

Another section through the trees leads to steps and a track. Turn left downhill and through a gate. At the road, turn left for a short distance until you reach the corner. Here, a path on the right descends through the trees to run alongside the Burn of Drum. Emerging at the Bridge of Dunnyduff, turn right to follow the road uphill to the outskirts of Keith. From here, keep following the signs for Keith Square.

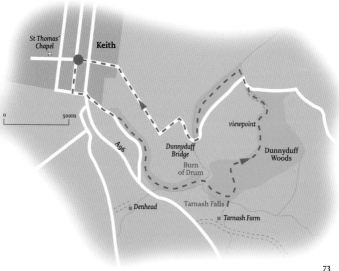

Fisher cottages at Crovie ▶

Heading further east, the wide sandy beaches of Moray give way to an increasingly rugged coastline featuring castles, caves and seabird colonies, as well as sandy coves and picturesque fishing villages. This corner of Scotland, often overlooked by visitors, rewards with an interesting cross-section of modern and old, gentrified and workaday, where you'll still hear the distinctive Doric dialect.

The old county town of Banff has scores of fascinating and well-preserved buildings. On its fringes is Duff House, an elegant, Adam-designed palatial pad in lovely parkland; it houses an offshoot of the National Galleries of Scotland with ever-changing art exhibitions. All along the coast are fascinating towns and villages, many of which would make a great holiday base. Portsoy, to the west of Banff, has two elaborate stone-built harbours, one dating from the 17th century, and is home to the annual Scottish Traditional Boat Festival. Heading east are the much-photographed former fishing villages of Gardenstown, Crovie and Pennan, the latter immortalised in the classic film *Local Hero*. Further still is the town of Fraserburgh – today, the most important fishing port of them all.

Troup Head

Kinnard Head

① Portsoy
Banff ② ③ Macduff
④
Crovie ⑤ ⑥ Pennan
Gardenstown ⑦
Rosehearty
Fraserburgh ⑧ ⑨
Inverallochy
⑩ St Combs
Rattray Head

A98

A947

A98

A952

A90

Aberchirder

Turriff

A950

Peterhead

Oldmeldrum

Ellon

North Aberdeenshire

y and Sandend circuit

Distance 9km **Time** 3 hours
Terrain straightforward route with good paths on coast, farm tracks and minor roads **Map** OS Explorer 425
Access bus from Cullen and Banff on the Inverness-Aberdeen route

Portsoy's fascinating past as the centre of the local marble and herring trade is reflected in its beautiful buildings and two historic harbours. This circular walk skirts along the coast to visit the sandy beach at Sandend before returning through farmland.

Start from Portsoy's Old Harbour which is signed from the upper part of the town. Whilst there is some parking here, it is usually easier to use the car park in the eastern part of town near the caravan park and make the short walk past the New Harbour to the start point. The Old Harbour has double protection piers, built from vertically-set stones to give it extra resilience against the pounding of the sea. After it was built in 1692, Portsoy expanded to become a major port, exporting Portsoy Marble (actually serpentine, although it has a marbled look), linen and coal, as well as supporting a fishing industry. Such was the importance of the herring and salmon boom locally that a new harbour was built in 1825. The tall poles used for drying nets can still be seen near this

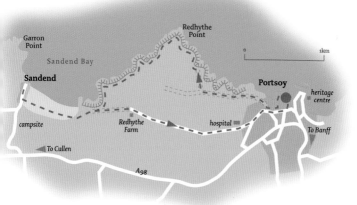

harbour, and there is an exhibition on Portsoy's heritage in the old icehouse opposite, known today as the Salmon Bothy.

From the Old Harbour, walk a very short way up North High Street and take the path on the right signed for West Braes. This climbs to give good views over the roofs to the two harbours before curving around the clifftop. Pass some houses on the left and, at a junction, continue straight ahead and then keep left to follow the coastal path, looking down on the disused seawater bathing pool below.

On meeting a road, walk left and, beyond the passing area, bear right along a track past a house. Shortly after, take the grassy track on the right marked with an arrow. The clifftop is gained once more at an old Second World War building; turn left and follow the coast. A short detour

to the right after a couple of minutes reveals an impressive natural arch.

Where the path forks, you could take the seaward path out to the headland which is a good spot for birdwatching. The main path shortcuts across the headland and continues on springy grass and heather. After a stile, turn right to head down to Sandend beach, passing a pillbox at the bottom. If you wish to visit the village, you can do so by crossing the sand.

To return, cross back over the sand and regain the coastal path. When you see a vehicle barrier ahead, continue past it on a grassy track aiming for Redhythe Farm. From here, just keep to the road, eventually passing the hospital on the outskirts of Portsoy. At the next junction, turn left to reach the main square and head back down North High Street to the Old Harbour.

◄ The Old Harbour, Portsoy

Whitehills circular

Terrain almost ... walk on clear paths, sandy beach, tracks and minor road
Map OS Explorer 425 Access bus to Banff on the Inverness-Aberdeen route

Explore the sandy beaches of the coastline stretching from historic Banff to the former fishing village of Whitehills. The walk has good opportunities for birdwatching and an ice cream shop for a fine summer day.

Start from the harbour car park in Banff, which is near the north pier and signed from the main street. Walk along the seawall heading west away from the harbour and the town, aiming for the row of houses at Scotstown. Look out for a series of rocks known as the Babes, which can be seen at low water. After the last cottage, turn sharp left to pass under the old railway line and follow the path up onto the former track, now a cycleway; keep heading west towards Boyndie Bay.

Once above the car park, walk down to it and then along a path to the beach. There are concrete steps down onto the sand; if the tide is very high, the track through the campsite can be taken instead. Cross the expanse of sand to the far end of the campsite and then leave the beach, crossing the site and bearing slightly right to a footbridge over the river. At the far side, the track runs along the shore. This

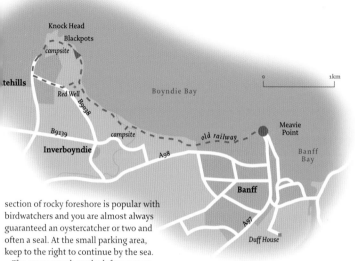

section of rocky foreshore is popular with birdwatchers and you are almost always guaranteed an oystercatcher or two and often a seal. At the small parking area, keep to the right to continue by the sea.

The caravan park on the left was once the site of a thriving brick and tileworks and is the source of the many seaworn bits of red brick that turn up on the nearby beaches. The bricks were then loaded into ships at the old harbour at Blackpots, the remains of which can be seen on the right. Nowadays, the small shop does a good trade in ice creams. Keep to the road as it winds past Knock Head to reach the harbour at Whitehills. Like most of the coastal settlements in Moray and Aberdeenshire, Whitehills was built on the back of the fishing industry and fishing vessels operated out of the harbour until 1999 when it was redeveloped as a leisure boat marina. If you do fancy returning with some of

today's catch, the large Downies fish factory has a shop with a wet fish counter. To reach it, carry on along the harbour road and it can be seen straight ahead.

To continue the walk, turn left uphill before the entrance to Downies. Near the top of the hill, take the second on the left, Loch Street, passing the toilets and a shop as you follow the residential street. Once past the last house but before the speed limit sign, turn down a small lane to return to the coast. Pass the Red Well, claimed to have healing properties and to date back to Roman times. At the bottom of the hill, the outward route is regained. Turn right to retrace the shore walk all the way back to Banff Harbour.

◀ Harbour wall at Blackpots

Banff Heritage Trail

Distance 3km **Time** 1 hour 30
Terrain waymarked with metal arrows set
into the paving stones **Map** OS Explorer
426 **Access** regular bus to Banff on the
Inverness-Aberdeen route

**Banff is a treasure trove of ancient
buildings and fascinating history – this
urban walk takes in the most interesting
features. An excellent route to combine
with a visit to the nearby gallery at Duff
House or Banff's wide sandy beach.**

Many of the oldest buildings here have
been restored by the Banff Preservation
and Heritage Society, which has also set
up this Heritage Trail; look out for the
numbered waymarkers set out into the
pavement and the blue plaques on the
buildings. Start from the pay and display
car park near the tourist information centre
on the south side of town; leaflets with
more information on the walk are available
here. Head uphill to the main road and bear

left to cross it beyond the barrier. Continue
up across Sandyhill Road and then turn
right in front of the old academy. Head up
the high street past numbers 31 to 39, good
examples of 18th-century Scottish
townhouses. Number 45, the Shoemakers'
building, has a grand stone archway.

Turn left after Forbes House (look for
the gargoyle), and take the next right to
view the courtyard of the Town and
Country Club, a large townhouse built in
1772 for a rich stocking manufacturer,
Provost Robinson. Return to the high
street and now cross at the crossing. The
trail goes back down the high street to see
the Georgian County Hotel and St
Brandon's, one of several houses linked
with Lord Byron's boyhood. Return to the
crossing, looking down the steep Strait
Path, where John Wesley preached to a
large crowd. From here, head down Old
Castlegate past some fine 18th-century
houses and turn left to regain the main

◀ Chalmers Hospital, Banff

road, now Castle Street, and turn right along it.

Bear right between the twin lodges guarding the entrance to Banff Castle, more of a stately home than a fortress. There are good views of the town of Macduff across the bay. Return to Castle Street and pass the medieval ruins of the true castle, taking the second left up Clunie Street in front of the ornate Chalmers Hospital. At the top, turn right into Fife Street and right again to pass Battery Green where volunteers manned gun emplacements against French privateers during the Napoleonic Wars, 1791-1815. Turn right at the corner of the Old Brewery, Banff's oldest industrial building, dating from 1705. Head left down the hill at the Railway Inn overlooking the harbour, once busy with herring boats but now housing a marina.

At the bottom, follow the road round to the right to reach the harbour and along the seafront to 11 Deveronside, the first house to be saved by the Preservation Society in the 1960s. Next door was the home of Thomas Edward, a shoemaker and renowned naturalist (see plaque). Eventually, bear left into Old Market Place to see the Meal House opposite, with the cupola from the old grammar school, now a restoration project. Turn right to reach Reid Street and then right and left once

more to reach the historic kirkyard. Two very impressive old, pink- and sandy-coloured houses are ahead on High Shore. Make the detour along High Shore and look up Water Path, then back into Low Street, past the Victorian Biggar Fountain opposite the Town House. Here stands the Mercat or Banff Town Cross, with a carving of the Virgin and Child. Keep on Low Street, passing the Court House on the right to return to the car park at the start of the trail.

Duff House and Bridge of Alvah

Distance 8.5km **Time** 2 hours 30
Terrain clear paths, tracks and minor road;
can be muddy **Maps** OS Explorer 425 and
426 **Access** nearest bus stop is at Banff,
1km away

**Leave behind the bustle of the coastline to
seek out the spectacular Bridge of Alvah
spanning the River Deveron. This pleasant
country walk leaves time to visit Duff
House or explore historic Banff.**

Duff House, just south of and within
walking distance of Banff, is a fabulous and
quite unexpectedly grand stately home.
Designed with a classical facade by William
Adam, it was completed in 1740 as the home
of the Earls of Fife after whom the house is
named. Since that time, the elegant walls

have played host to a number of uses,
including a hotel, sanatorium and prisoner
of war camp. Much of the house is now part
of the National Galleries of Scotland, with
permanent and visiting exhibitions, as well
as a café and shop. This walk explores the
former grounds, taking in the wooded
riverside, an icehouse and mausoleum, as
well as the Bridge of Alvah.

The walk begins from Duff House car
park, which is well signed from Banff.
Follow the track to the right of the playing
fields, signed for 'Woodland Walks and
Bridge of Alvah', to reach the Fife Gates.
Carry straight on into the woods, ignoring
the first path on the left. Keep left at a fork
and soon you'll see the icehouse, the smeg
fridge of its day, down on the left. Descend
the steps to visit it and then carry on down
to join a woodland path, turning right to
meander through the trees towards the

River Deveron. At a fork, go right to reach the mausoleum, built in 1793 with ornate stonework by the second Earl of Fife.

From here, join the track above and head left along it before bearing right when it meets another track. At the next junction, keep straight ahead to reach a bungalow and then turn left. There are open fields to the right and, further on, good views down to the river at times; keep left at another fork to drop downhill to the Bridge of Alvah. The spectacular single-arch stone bridge, set high above the river, dates from 1722. The River Deveron flows through deep pools far below at this point and is popular with salmon and trout fishermen during the season. It is also a good place to glimpse the flash of brilliant blue that signals a kingfisher.

Cross the bridge and keep on the track, branching left at a fork to pass above Montcoffer House. After this, the route bears left, passing the remains of a medieval doocot. Soon the track becomes a minor road and eventually reaches a T-junction. Turn left here and then left again just after a white cottage. As the track bends, take the path straight ahead between gorse and broom.

The path widens through the woods and, at Gaveney Cottage, there is a great view over Banff and the surrounding countryside. Carry straight on along the surfaced road, passing the MacDuff Distillery to emerge onto the main road. Head left along the pavement to the next junction and then left to cross Banff Bridge. Finally, turn left once more onto the driveway to Duff House and return to the car park.

◀ Duff House, Banff

Gardenstown and Crovie explorer

Distance 4.5km **Time** 2 hours
Terrain clear paths, coastal section may
not be passable at very high tide or in
stormy weather; minor roads, some with
pavements **Map** OS Explorer 426
Access bus from Banff and Fraserburgh
to Gardenstown

These two much photographed villages of
fishing cottages are linked by a short but
spectacular coastal path. After exploring
Crovie, a steep climb inland gives great
views on the way back to Gardenstown;
a further excursion leads to a ruined
church at the far end of the bay.

There is parking right down at the
bottom of Gardenstown – as long as you
can negotiate the hairpin bends, after

which the walk may seem easy! Head
down the steep hill, turning right at the
bottom and continue past the huts to
reach the parking area. From here, the
route starts across the small section of
sand (impossible for a short period at high
tide) and soon follows a path built closely
against the bottom of the cliff. Climb steps
and walk through a narrow gap in the
rocks to reveal the rest of the path to
Crovie – a tiny, picturesque cluster of
cottages cowering beneath high cliffs.

A cairn commemorates the heroic rescue
undertaken by the people of Gardenstown
and Crovie when the SS *Vigilant* ran
aground on rocks here during a storm in

1906. Villagers successfully rescued the entire crew despite the violent February seas. When Crovie is reached, the route continues up the tarmac road to the right, but it is well worth wandering along the seafront to explore this tiny village where the main street is only wide enough for pedestrians. Even on a calm day, it is easy to imagine the battering these cottages receive during storms and to understand why they are built with their gable ends facing the water.

Once you have explored Crovie, take the only road out of the village which climbs very steeply. Pass the residents' car park and continue to a larger parking area with a picnic spot on the right. There is a wooden sculpture of a woman staring out to sea; this is a great viewpoint over the bay. From here, the road makes the more gentle climb to a junction; turn right to reach the upper end of Gardenstown. At the main road, nearly opposite the shop, turn right to descend the steep road, going left at the fork to reach the seafront. This older part of the village is known as Seatown; its narrow alleys and lanes are well worth exploring on foot.

At the far western end of the village, take the ramp down onto the sand and cross the beach. Look out for a grassy glen and take the path up it. Near the top, the path curves right and reaches a ruined cottage and then the graveyard. The ruined church, which dates from 1513, was built long before the village it overlooks and is dedicated to St John the Evangelist. From here, return to Gardenstown by the same route and continue past the harbour to the car park.

◀ Crovie

85

Troup Head from Crovie

Distance **9km** Time **3 hours 30**
Terrain **farm tracks, some steep sections, rough paths and minor roads, one long flight of steps** Map **OS Explorer 426**
Access **nearest bus stop is at Gardenstown, 500m walk from Crovie**

Combine the best of the north Aberdeenshire coast on this circular walk from the picturesque village of Crovie. The objective is Troup Head, known for its high cliffs and large gannet colony.

The curved line of cottages, huddled hard against the looming hillside, end-on to the sea, is familiar from postcards and calendars. Crovie (pronounced 'Crivvy') was built as a fishing village in the cramped space between the sea and the steep ground behind. Its population was boosted by the Highland Clearances in the late 19th century when as many as 300 people lived here, clawing a living from the sea. In 1953, a huge storm wreaked havoc, destroying many houses and

causing the local authority to consider razing the remainder of the village. A long campaign against this proposal succeeded and the village now has protected status. Although the fishermen have long since gone, the harbour remains at the far end of the village and the main street is only wide enough for a couple of people, liable to be splashed by the waves at high tide.

Parking at Crovie itself is restricted to residents and those staying here, and in any case the drive down the final hairpin bends is not recommended. It is, therefore, best to start from the viewpoint car park on the left as you approach the village.

From here, walk down the road and a steep flight of steps on the right to reach the village. From the bottom, Crovie can be explored in both directions before returning to the burn at the centre. Keep to the right-hand side as you face inland and take the narrow track, soon crossing the water to pass in front of two cottages before the track climbs steeply. At the top,

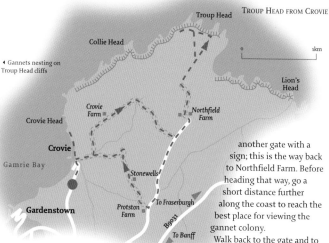

◄ Gannets nesting on
Troup Head cliffs

turn left and continue uphill. After the
bend, take the track marked with a green
arrow on the left and follow this past
Crovie Farm and then on to reach the road
near the entrance to Northfield Farm.

Turn left here to begin a detour to
Troup Head, where you'll find mainland
Scotland's only gannet colony. With more
than 1500 of these large, distinctive
seabirds, these cliffs are particularly
impressive during the spring. A live CCTV
feed also allows you to view pictures of
the nesting birds from the aquarium in
Banff. The track beyond Northfield Farm
leads to a parking area, where you then
keep right at the fork. When the route
forks at the far end of a field, take the
right option to eventually reach a kissing
gate giving access to the cliff edge. Skirt
along this to the left, taking great care as
the edge is unprotected. Ignore a gate in
the fence on the left and continue to

another gate with a
sign; this is the way back
to Northfield Farm. Before
heading that way, go a
short distance further
along the coast to reach the
best place for viewing the
gannet colony.

Walk back to the gate and to
Northfield Farm, returning to the
junction where you came up from
the right earlier. For an alternative route
back to Crovie, continue straight ahead on
the road, passing a pottery on the right
and then climbing to Protston Farm.
Opposite the barn on the left and before
the farmhouse, turn right down a rough
track. Follow this through a right-angle
bend and aim for Stonewells Farm on the
right. After passing the farmhouse, go
straight ahead onto a grassy track,
keeping the barn on the right. The path
drops downhill between field fences
which are replaced by gorse as it curves
to the left into the floor of a glen. This soon
emerges near the bungalow seen earlier in
the walk. Aim straight ahead down the
track and turn the corner, retracing the
outward route down the track on the right
to Crovie and the steep climb back up to
the car park.

Pennan to Aberdour Bay

Distance 7km Time 1 hour 30 (one way)
Terrain clear coastal path, farm tracks and
minor road, some navigation needed
Map OS Explorer 426 Access bus from Banff
and Fraserburgh to Pennan; no public
transport from Aberdour Bay

A visit to the sandstone arches and caves
of Aberdour Bay is a must for visitors to
the area – this linear walk heads to the bay
from the picturesque village of Pennan,
immortalised in the 1980's film *Local Hero*.
Transport needs to be arranged, or the
route can be reversed for the return.

Pennan consists of a line of cottages
tightly squeezed between the cliffs and
the sea, presenting their gable ends to the

winter storms. Although the storms are
still a regular threat, in recent years it is
landslips from the cliffs behind that have
caused havoc. A large chunk of the
unstable cliff has now been removed.
There is a parking area at the western end
of the village near the community hall.
Start with a lovely walk along the front by
the houses, with their drying lines on the
other side of the path. Continue to the
Pennan Hotel and the red phonebox
immortalised in the 1983 film *Local Hero*.
The phonebox in the film was actually a
prop, but so many people came expecting
to see it that a real one was installed in
the village.

At the harbour, pass the last house and

head inland on a path signed for Aberdour. It climbs steeply and is hemmed in by high hedges until, after a gate, it comes to a field. Stay close to the fence, aiming for the farm buildings on the horizon. Looking back, the distinctive shape of Troup Head juts out into the sea. Cross the stile and keep left of the barns, going straight ahead at the crossroads and through a farm gate onto a track. Further on, when the track bends right, take the track straight on through a gate (footpath sign). The route now rises through the rolling farmland to emerge at a road. Turn left for a short distance before taking a signed track to the left at a corner. Follow the track past a small loch and over a stile; the first views of Aberdour Bay are revealed below.

As the track begins to descend, look out for a path on the right signed with the Nortrail logo. After a short section between gorse bushes, this path emerges on a track; continue ahead past farm buildings and across the bottom of the valley before climbing the far side. At the road, turn left to pass the churchyard and reach Aberdour Bay.

The drama of the spectacular nearby caves and arches is not immediately apparent. Head to the right across the grass and then up the track above the cliff. Keep on the main path to bear left, taking the easiest route down into the next bay. Here, a massive arch can be explored, worn into the red sandstone by the power of the sea and a favourite roost of birds. At low tide, you can walk back through this arch and work your way through another two natural arches to return to Aberdour Bay. This route is completely covered by water at high tide, so keep an eye on the sea. If tide and time allow, there are more sea caves to investigate further along the coast.

Fraserburgh Bay and Waters of Philorth

Distance 7.5km **Time** 2 hours
Terrain sandy beach or dunes, grassy
path and track **Map** OS Explorer 427
Access Fraserburgh is well served by buses

**Stroll along Fraserburgh's bright and
breezy esplanade and the seemingly
endless sand of Fraserburgh Bay. When
the sands do run out, this route heads
inland through a nature reserve before
returning through the dunes.**

The town of Fraserburgh is dominated
by the sea and fishing. It rapidly
expanded at the start of the herring boom
in 1815 and remains a major white fish
port, with 60 percent of the population
dependent on fishing in some way for
their living. It is also one of the places you
are most likely to hear expressions in
Doric, the northeastern dialect. Most

common is the expression 'fit like',
meaning 'how are you?' Doric can be so
incomprehensible to outsiders that the
BBC TV series, *Trawlermen*, about life on
the ocean-going fishing boats was
subtitled into English.

To the south of the town is a wide
expanse of award-winning beach; this
walk starts from the Esplanade car park at
its northern end; it is signed from the
A90. Head straight out onto the sands and
bear right towards the immense strip of
dunes. Soon a burn is crossed; this is
usually possible on the lower part of the
beach, but at high tides it may be
necessary to go up to the sea wall and
cross there. The route now carries on
along the beach, unless the tide is very
high in which case the going will be
rougher amongst the dunes.

◀ Fraserburgh along the sands

After a long section along the beach, the harbour and point of Cairnbulg can be seen on the other side of the Water of Philorth. The wreck of the *Sovereign* can be seen jutting out of the water just off the coast. The fishing vessel hit the rocks in December 2005, was holed in several places and was deemed beyond salvage so has remained a landmark and a warning to shipping ever since.

When you reach the Water of Philorth, turn right and shadow it inland, using a boardwalk on the right after a short distance to take a path through the dunes adjacent to the river. This is part of the Waters of Philorth Nature Reserve and is a great place to spot waders such as heron, oystercatcher, sanderling or dunlin. On meeting a fence, keep to the right of it and follow a boardwalk to a junction. The left boardwalk heads to the nature reserve car park, but to return to Fraserburgh bear right to take the path up through the dunes and then back down onto the beach. Once on the sand, turn left to retrace your steps to the start, with the profile of Fraserburgh drawing closer – the promise of fish and chips may encourage a spring in your step.

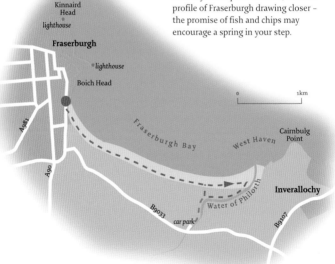

Cairnbulg Point and Whitelinks Bay

Distance **6km** Time **2 hours**
Terrain **tracks, path through dunes and
sandy beach** Map **OS Explorer 427**
Access **regular bus from St Combs and
Fraserburgh to Inverallochy**

**The tightly packed cottages of Cairnbulg
and Inverallochy feature on this walk
which heads out onto the wind-blown
sands before returning through dunes and
the golf course.**

Cairnbulg and Inverallochy's fishing
cottages were built, like many in the area,
end on to the sea with only a small
window in the gable end providing a view
of the water. This claustrophobic design
protected the houses from the worst of
the storms, whilst making the most use
of the limited space near the sea. The best
place to park is near the harbour to the

north. Start the walk by returning along
the sea road past the Lookout House,
remaining beside the water along Shore
Street with its numerous drying lines
facing the water.

If time allows, it is worth visiting
Maggie's Hoosie, a tiny whitewashed
cottage with a red pan-tiled roof. This
belonged to Maggie Duthie who lived in it
until 1950, and it has since been preserved
as an example of a typical But 'n' Ben
fisherman's cottage and is open most
afternoons. The cottage consists of two
rooms, with the attic rafters being used to
store nets, creels and other fishing
paraphernalia. The But would have been
reserved for special occasions and
entertaining whilst the Ben was used for
communal living and sleeping. With no
running water, a range was used to heat

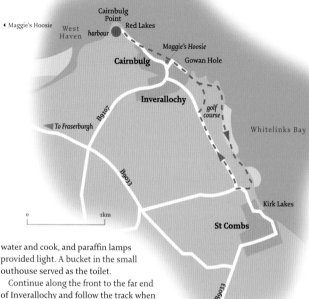

water and cook, and paraffin lamps provided light. A bucket in the small outhouse served as the toilet.

Continue along the front to the far end of Inverallochy and follow the track when the road curves inland. At a turning area, take the grassy path between the golf course and the coast, soon heading down the dunes to reach the beach at Whitelinks Bay. This lovely sandy beach is usually very quiet. Signs of a less peaceful time are apparent from the concrete anti-tank blocks and other fortifications from WWII that lie at angles in the centre of the beach. The northeast coast was considered a prime target for a German land invasion and a defensive line of military installations was put in place along it.

Carry on along the beach until you are opposite a stone boat enclosure. Take the track inland from here, taking care as it cuts across the golf course, and bear right onto the minor road beyond. At a bend, go right again onto a tarmac lane which runs beside the golf course to return to Inverallochy. After passing many grand modern houses, branch right at the fork to pass the clubhouse and take one of the narrow streets to the seafront, eventually returning to the start at the harbour.

St Combs and Strathbeg Nature Reserve

**Distance 6.75km Time 2 hours 30
Terrain sandy beach and dunes
Map OS Explorer 427 Access regular bus
from Fraserburgh and Inverallochy**

**Discover part of one of Scotland's biggest
dune systems on this trip into the
Strathbeg Nature Reserve from the
village of St Combs.**

St Combs is a small fishing village
dating back to 1785. When the village was
established by the local landowner,
residents were given £5 to build their
houses to a plan. The result is a neat
layout of near identical houses facing
away from the sea. There is a parking area
just to the east of the village on the track
to the Tufted Duck Hotel. To reach it, turn
off the main road in St Combs at a right-
angle bend near St Columba's Church,

following signs for the hotel. The parking
is on the left before the hotel is reached.

Walk back to St Columba's, which gives
the village its name, and turn right after
the church into Church Street. Before the
public toilets, turn right along a track next
to the high wall of the cemetery. Continue
straight ahead when another track joins,
and follow it through the dunes to a
rough turning area.

From here, you'll find access to the beach
and, unless the tide is very high, you can
cross the sands to the right. The massive
dune system stretches all the way to Rattray
Head, the lighthouse of which can be seen
in the distance, and beyond. The waters are
popular with grey seals at all times of year
and, in the summer months, pods of
bottlenose dolphins pass each week as they
head to and from the Moray Firth.

◄ Barefoot on the beach, St Combs

After 2km along the sands, you'll come to the outflow from the Loch of Strathbeg. Turn right here to head inland around the edge of a lagoon, a popular spot for wading birds. Keep to the edge of the lagoon and, when necessary, climb the steep dune to join a rough path running along the top. Follow this to the left, keeping an eye out for treacherous hidden rabbit holes which could cause a broken leg or a humiliating headfirst tumble.

Loch Strathbeg is seen ahead. This is Britain's largest dune loch and a haven for overwintering birds when thousands of swans, ducks and geese fly in. Although not accessible from the walk, it is worth making a trip to the RSPB visitor centre and hides just north of Crimond. It is especially spectacular from late September to March when the loch is home to one-fifth of the world's population of pink-footed geese – an awesome sight when they come in to roost.

The faint path follows the river upstream until it reaches a bridge. Do not cross but instead turn right, taking a clear path next to a drainage channel which runs all the way through the dunes back

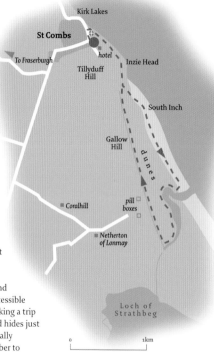

to St Combs. The line of pill boxes on the right were built as defences against invasion from the sea and show how far the sands have shifted. Ignore a track down to the beach and, at the next junction, bear left to return up past the cemetery to Church Road. Turn left and left again to reach the parking area.

Index